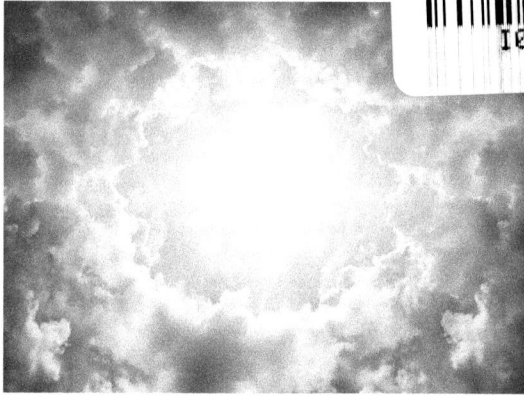

The 70th-Week & Rapture Parallels

A **WORD** to the Watchful and a **WARNING** to the Wayward

David Wayne Meeker

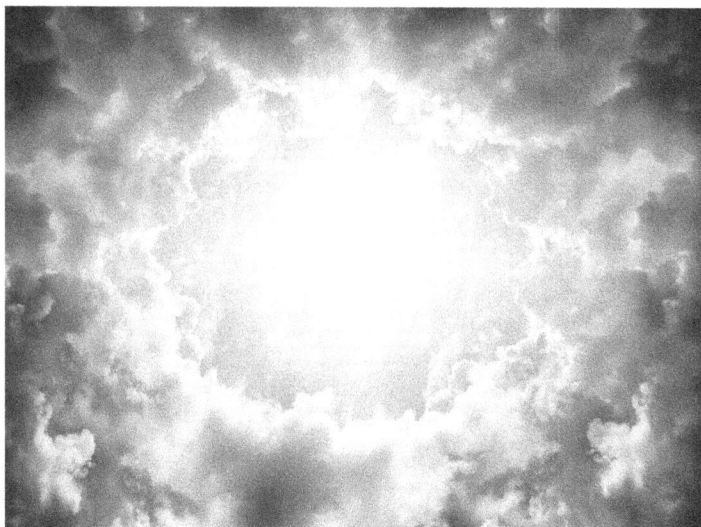

The 70th-Week & Rapture Parallels

A **WORD** to the Watchful and a **WARNING** to the Wayward

David Wayne Meeker

LAST CHANCE

Published by Last Chance Music Ministry

ELEVATION PRESS
OF COLORADO

The 70th-Week & Rapture Parallels:
A WORD to the Watchful and a WARNING to the Wayward

By David Wayne Meeker

Copyright © 2023. All rights reserved worldwide.

Published by Last Chance Music Ministry, Hutto, Texas.
Preliminary and general editing services provided by Laura Diane Meeker.
Cover design and interior design and formatting by Elevation Press of Colorado.
Front cover photo by Pernsanit/Freepik.
Back cover photo courtesy of Laura Diane Meeker.
Some charts adapted from https://prewrathresources.wordpress.com/free-pre-wrath-charts/
All rights reserved. Used by permission.

All Scriptures are *The Holy Bible, Berean Study Bible, BSB.*
©2016, 2018 by Bible Hub, unless otherwise noted.
Used by permission.

Elevation Press
P.O. Box 603
Cedaredge, CO 81413

Ordering information: Quantity sales. Special discounts are available on quantity purchases by book clubs, corporations, associations, and others. For details, contact the publisher at the address above.

ISBN 979-8-9853834-3-0

1. Main category—[Bible] 2. Other categories—[End Time Prophecy]—[Apologetics]—[Eschatology]

© 2023
Last Chance Music Ministry
lastchancemusic1@aol.com

Elevation Press of Colorado
Cedaredge, Colorado
www.elevation-press-books.com

Acknowledgements

To Robert Van Kampen and Marvin Rosenthal:
Thank you for having the courage to tell me the truth.

The 70th-Week & Rapture Parallels
is lovingly dedicated to our grandchildren.

Contents

Introduction

My book, *The 70th-Week & Rapture Parallels* is a WORD to the watchful and a WARNING to the wayward. First, let me tell you a little bit about my personal pre-tribulation journey. I had been a part of the pre-tribulation Rapture community since the day of my justification, through Jesus Christ, in the late '80s. I was taught the position by a well-respected and beloved Bible teacher from California. My mother, my father, and my church family also prescribed to the pre-tribulation Rapture position. I assumed for all those years that the pre-tribulation Rapture view was a Biblically accurate exegetical position. Everyone around me seemed to agree with the presuppositions of this view. From the time of my conversion to this most recently, it's been taught to me and the world via Christian radio, television, and the internet. There have been bestselling books written on the pre-tribulation topic, which have been sold in multiple millions of dollars annually. There have also been movies created based on this topic that are being produced and viewed in theaters all around the globe. Although aware of all this, through my pre-tribulation Rapture experience, I never thought to systematically study the topic for myself. I just took — by faith — the words of many trusted and respected men and women within the Body of Christ, but over the years, even before I started studying the specifics about the most popular tribulation Rapture topics seriously for myself, there were two major fundamental issues that did not quite fit properly within my Biblical hermeneutical mindset. These two fundamental issues are as follows:

1. The pre-tribulation and mid-tribulation communities present Jesus Christ coming to Earth a total of three times (once invisibly and twice visibly), not just twice visibly, as Scriptures clearly indicate.

2. They use obvious physical Second Coming of Christ, and Bodily Resurrection passages, after removing them from their originally intended context, and then use them as a pre-text, in proving the Biblical legitimacy of their eschatological positions (i.e. invisible Rapture).

Recently, I came across statements by the late Dr. John Walvoord, the former president of Dallas Theological Seminary, who emphatically held to the pre-tribulation view. In contrast to his current view, an early edition of his book, The Rapture Question, contains the assertion that neither post-tribulationism nor pre-tribulationism are explicit teachings of the Scriptures. He further declares that the Bible does not explicitly refer to either. His statements which deny that either position is supported by Scripture appeared in the first edition of The Rapture Question but were removed from the subsequent edition. To my mind, this removal demonstrates what length some proponents of the pre-tribulation movement are willing to go to promote a non-Biblically substantiated position. Through my research, I found that historically, the belief in a secret and invisible Rapture is a relatively new teaching that was not taught by Jesus, the Prophet Daniel, the Apostle Paul, or the Apostle John, and the pre-tribulation and mid-tribulation views are being taught as plausible positions without Biblical justification. Also, it turns out that not only has God's Word always taught that the Second Coming of Christ would be a literal and physically loud, and noisy event, not invisible, but that it will also be Glorious and Magnificent — again, not silent and invisible. Also, through my preliminary research, I learned that the Church, in general, have always believed that the Rapture would occur after the Church would endure severe persecution, brought about through the work of the anti-Christ. These people include John Bunyan, John Calvin, Jonathan Edwards, Matthew Henry, Charles Finney, John Huss, John Knox, C. S. Lewis, Martin Luther, George Mueller, John Newton, Charles Spurgeon, William Tyndale, Isaac Watts, Charles Wesley, John Wesley, John Wycliffe, Ulrich Zwingli, and many others. After this previously unknown information was discovered, I had a desire to learn more about the what, where, when, why, and how concerning the teachings of Daniel's 70th Week and its surrounding parallel passages. Once I began to seriously study the details of these various events, I became quite amazed by the Pre-Wrath view's Scriptural support, in particular, with how every aspect of this view fits perfectly into place, like pieces of a puzzle. As a result of this study, I now believe the Pre-Wrath Rapture position is the most correct Biblical view on this subject, and I want to share with you why I believe this. If you want to know what the Scriptures actually teach about the Beginning of Sorrows (i.e. birth pains), the Great Tribulation, the Rapture, the Resurrection, the Second Coming of Christ, and the End of the Age, then you should read my book, *The 70th-Week & Rapture Parallels*. The reason I have a desire to share this information with you is that I now have a better understanding about the Biblical truth surrounding these topics, and I think you should, too! I did feel at first that I had been misled by certain people within my denomination, which I had trusted and respected for so many years; but then I understood the misinterpretations made about these majorly important Biblical events are secondary issues and the Biblical misinterpretations were made by sincere, loving, and caring people from within the Body of Christ, and were not a deliberate act of deception but instead, I believe, these were just honest misinterpretations on a very difficult and complicated topic. I think we need to show the men and women of the Body of Christ who mistranslated these majorly important end-of-times prophecies love and grace. We are not to divide over the differences found within our eschatological interpretations. In other words, the timing of the Rapture and Tribulation is not a salvation issue. We need to remember we are all fallen creations, and none of us is perfect — *no, not one.* Only the Triune God is perfect. As the elect, we do not want to get distracted away from our true calling and commission in this life — which is to preach the Gospel of Jesus Christ to a lost and dying world. When I understood the level of Biblical accuracy surrounding the Pre-wrath Rapture position and how it all fits perfectly together exegetically, while implementing the well-established rules of Biblical hermeneutics, I discovered that the Pre-Wrath position fits better with the Biblical worldview than any of the other popular competing views, with regard to its consistency and unity with all the Bible passages and their parallels, in their correct context — such as Daniel's 70th Week; Jesus' Olivet Discourse; prophecies in the Book of Matthew; the writings of the Apostle Paul in First and Second Thessalonians; the Book of Joel; the Book of Revelation; and many other passages that I will be sharing with you later in this book. When I discovered the Biblical truth about these events, I must be honest with you, this experience also made me feel as though I had been a bit Biblically naive for believing that I could have somehow obtained a free ticket, or great escape pass, prior to the future arrival of the horrific persecution and tribulation events coming to Earth. I think one of the reasons I was feeling I had been naive was for thinking I would personally escape death and persecution, while most of the Apostles, the Disciples, and multiple hundreds of thousands of other believers from the First-Century Church to the present Church age have been gruesomely and horribly martyred — for the sake of Christ. Did I think somehow, I could escape death and persecution, even though the Holy Bible has declared to me precisely what I would have to endure as an end-time believer in a chronological sequence, during that last seven years of the current world's existence? God revealed in advance all of the details of the Last Days to me that I needed to know, but as I read Scripture, I understand better today that Biblical Christianity and following Christ is essentially a death sentence to oneself. What I mean by that statement is that dying to self for Christ's sake is an absolute surrender to God. Jesus taught His disciples that whoever wants to save his or her life will lose it, but whoever loses his or her life for Jesus' sake will find it. In other words, nothing in this life is worth passing up the free gift of eternal life God offers us. This truth should have been of no surprise to me because as I read Matthew 16:24, I see that Christ told His Disciples if you want to be His disciple, you must, deny yourselves and carry your cross. I see examples of this throughout Scripture as I read the historically accurate stories found in the Biblical accounts that mention how Stephen was stoned to death, Paul was beheaded, and Church History tells us that James was beheaded, Matthew was killed by an axe, Mathias was both stoned and beheaded, Thomas was speared to death, and Peter was crucified upside-down. I could go on and on, but you get my point. So, I asked myself this question: "Why did I not understand the logical-outworking of my Pre-Tribulation position more clearly — relative to God's Holy Word — for all those many years, as I was moving forward through my sanctification process?" I think the reason for my lack of understanding on this topic was simply due to my lack of Biblical knowledge on this topic. Did I think I had more obedience and commitment to God in my life than these great men of God: Apostle Paul, Apostle Mark, Apostle Matthew, or Apostle James? Again, I think not! Most of these God-honoring men were martyred for Christ's sake. Did I — as a follower of Christ — believe I deserved less persecution from the world and Satan than these mighty men of God did? Again, I think not! If you're looking to get your ears tickled, or to obtain an in-depth study on the Book of Revelation, or if you want to read a fictitious story about the great escape at the end of the Church age, or a fictitious story about the End-Times Church who will receive less persecution by men and Satan than its previous First-Century Church and current believers have receive — if this is in fact what you are craving, then I think you probably will not enjoy this book and you should not waste your time reading it. If you are looking for truth about Daniel's 70th Week; the Beginning of Sorrows; the Birth Pains; the Great Tribulation that Christ, John, and Daniel spoke about; and if you are looking for the truth with regard to the correct timing of the Rapture of the Church, at the End of the Age, then for these reasons I think you should read my book *The 70th-Week & Rapture Parallels.* When I finally began to study the Scriptures on these Rapture-related topics, I found major inconsistencies and contextual issues with the most popular Tribulation and Rapture theories; but during my exegetical studies on the End- of-the-Age prophecies, I found some unexpected parallel information you will probably not believe, or rather, should I say, you will find it hard to believe. None the less — due to the importance of this information — I have no choice but to share this information with you, my brothers and sisters, whom I love in Christ, so you can be better prepared for the coming tribulation and persecution that is quickly headed our way. What I discovered in my research, I now want to share with you in my new book — *The 70th-Week & Rapture Parallels* — so you can prepare yourself to share this information with others; but before you start reading my book, I want you to know that the information I will be sharing with you in this book is not intended to be divisive but is intended for the

Bereans found within the Body of Christ (Ac. 17:11) who love God's Word and want to know what the Holy Bible actually teaches us about the Rapture of the Church and the related events surrounding this topic (Rev. 1:3). The main reason I am writing this book to the Body of Christ is that I understand the importance of this topic, which is that if the Church is going to go through the Beginning of Sorrows (i.e. birth pains) and the Great Tribulation, then the Church will need to be prepared to endure these events and to help others to prepare as well. I want you to understand that I strongly believe the Holy Bible teaches the Pre-Wrath Rapture view and eventually this view will probably become the most prominent view within the Body of Christ in the not-so-far-off future. It is already spreading like a wildfire among the Bereans. Please keep in mind all of the different End-Time theories circulating around in the Church today are considered to be secondary issues, and Christians should never divide over secondary issues. Secondary issues have nothing to do with salvation and are not a necessity but an accessory. We can lovingly disagree but never divide. Dividing over a secondary issue is more of a sin against God than the actual prophetic disagreement itself, and we would do well to heed this truth.

At this time, I would like to explain to you the reason for the method of study used in this book. The method of study is called *Passage Parallels*. The reason for the *Passage-Parallels* study method is that I want to let God tell His Own story — through His Word — not my words. I will be using this method of study found in the rules of Biblical Hermeneutics (i.e. The Art and Science of Biblical Interpretation) called *Passage Parallels*. By using this method of study, we will be letting God both speak and interpret in His Own Words. Let me explain. For example, first I identify a specific passage for study, which we will call (A), and second, I search for its parallel passage of the same context and content, which we will call (B). Once I have identified that it is the same context and content in passage (A) as in (B), then I extract any additional previously unknown information from *Parallel Passage* (B) and add that information to *Parallel Passage* (A), whereby creating a greater understanding, or broader picture, of the events in question. So, let's begin our exegetical adventure, and discover the Biblical truth about the Beginning of Sorrows, the Great Tribulation, the Cosmic Disturbance, the Rapture of the Elect, the Second Coming of Christ, and the Day of the Lord. I believe that what we believe about these above-mentioned topics will affect how we live our life for Christ. My purpose in writing *The 70th-Week & Rapture Parallels* is not to divide the Body of Christ but rather to unite us. It is my desire that after you finish reading my book, *The 70th-Week & Rapture Parallels*, you will be better prepared to endure the most traumatic and difficult time of persecution and tribulation the Nation of Israel, the followers of Jesus Christ, and the deceived and misguided occupants of this world will ever experience; but thanks be to God for cutting the Great Tribulation short for the sake of the elect! Sometime near the end of the Great Tribulation, the Holy Bible tells us there will be a Cosmic Disturbance that will occur that will cut short the Great Tribulation, for the sake of the elect (Seal 6). According to the Scriptures, this will occur just prior to the Rapture of the Elect, and the Second Coming of Jesus Christ, and the Bodily Resurrection. These moments will be by far the most Magnificent and Spectacular Moments in the history of human reality. In my book, *The 70th-Week & Rapture Parallels*, I will be attempting to communicate the prophetic truths contained in God's Holy Word to you. I believe the key to understanding the many End-of-the-Age prophecies is solely contingent upon our correct understanding of Daniel's 70th Week. That is because Daniel's 70th Week is actually a Divine chronological sequencing tool which is historically and mathematically accurate in its chronological sequencing calculations of the current Earth's final seven-year period. It's so encouraging to know that God is working on the elect's behalf — both Jewish and Christian — during The 70th-Week-of-Daniel period. I will be showing you in my book, *The 70th-Week & Rapture Parallels*, the Biblical parallel passages found in Jesus' Olivet Discourse Prophecies from Matthew 24 and Luke 21, and also the Apostle Paul's parallels in 1 Thessalonians 4-5 and 2 Thessalonians 1-2, and the Apostle John's Book of Revelation 6-8. Then we can create a more comprehensive understanding of the events in question as I parallel the above-mentioned passages with Daniel's 70th Week in order to understand and accurately determine the Divine sequences in their precise chronological order. Also, I will be including two of the most unprecedented current political and financial events, which includes the aggressive seven-year Agenda 30 Sustainable Development Goals (SDG7), previously known as Agenda 21 of 1992, which has been signed by 193 United Nation member states. Also, we will take a look at the BRICS International Financial Treaty of 2015. In my book, *The 70th-Week & Rapture Parallels*, I will explain to you how these currently relevant, political, financial, and Biblical events parallel perfectly together with the many prophecies found in Scripture, and how the above-combined paralleled events will indeed affect your life, not only at this present time during the final seven years upon the current earth, but also your eternity as well. Also, in my book, *The 70th-Week & Rapture Parallels*, due to the premises and conclusions formed in this book, the validity of three of the four most popular Rapture views mentioned in this book will come into question for obvious logical reasons. Because of this, I will be going through an exercise called "process of elimination." First, I need to bring to your attention that I will not be using the four most popular Rapture views mentioned in this book to interpret these events found in Scripture, but rather I will be using Scripture to verify the validity of the four most popular Rapture views; then once a specific Rapture view has been verified through Scripture, then and only then, can we select the Rapture view that best corresponds with the passage relative to God's Word. I will be using the 70th Week of Daniel as the foundation text for determining the chronological sequencing to accurately identify specific event parallels and chronological orders within the last seven years of our current human history as they are revealed to us via information provided by Jesus in His Olivet Discourse Prophecies and Apostle John's Book of Revelation 6-8 and Apostle Paul's 1 and 2 Thessalonians. Now I want to direct your attention to the process of elimination exercise that I mentioned previously. I want to explain to you what I meant when I used the phrase *process of elimination*. If the conclusions formed within this book are correct, and if the signing of the covenant between the anti-Christ, the Nation of Israel, and the many, was September 18-19, 2023, (or its effective date), then my conclusions are as follows:

1. If the *Pre-Tribulation-Rapture* event does not occur before, or near, the covenant signing effective start date, then the *Pre-Tribulation-Rapture* view is false.

2. If the *Mid-Tribulation-Rapture* event does not occur at the 3½-year midpoint, beginning from the signing of the covenant's effective start date, then the *Mid-Tribulation-Rapture* view is false.

3. If the *Pre-Wrath-Rapture* event does occur after the Cosmic Disturbance at the sixth Seal, then the *Pre-Wrath-Rapture* view is correct, and the *Post-Tribulation-Rapture* view is false.

4. If the *Pre-Wrath-Rapture* view does not occur after the Cosmic Disturbance at the sixth Seal, then the *Pre-Wrath-Rapture* view is false, and the *Post-Tribulation-Rapture* view is correct.

My book, *The 70th-Week & Rapture Parallels*, can be used — in real time — as a Chronological Reference Guide as we go through the 70th Week of Daniel through this seven-year time span as indicated by Scripture as it parallels with the SDG7. If my calculations are correct, the 70th Week of Daniel began on September 18-19, 2023 (or effective date) — based on the United Nation aggressive SDG7 seven-year agreement effective-date time frame. I believe God's Word is so accurate and precise that we will be able to chronologically sequence the information revealed to us through God's Word as it is revealed through this book — *The 70th-Week & Rapture Parallels*. We will be able to follow along precisely in real time while we identify the exact sequencing of these Biblical events relative to Daniel's 70th Week and mentioned in multiple parallel passages found within the Holy Bible, as we compare them with the United Nation Agenda 30 and their 17 Sustainable Development Goals for the next — and last — seven years on the current Earth. My book, *The 70th-Week & Rapture Parallels*, is a WORD to the watchful and a WARNING to the wayward, and I have a word for both the watchful and the wayward:

- To the WATCHFUL (i.e. the elect): The time is beyond short for the non-believer. We must stand up and be counted. Now is the time to reach a lost and dying world with the Gospel of Jesus Christ before the opportunity passes.

- To the WAYWARD (i.e. the unrepentant): REPENT – BELIEVE – ABIDE. "Today is the day of salvation" –2 Corinthians 6:2. Before this opportunity passes, submit to the Work of the Holy Spirit in your life and come to the saving knowledge of Jesus Christ and you will be saved.

Let's begin the 70th Week of Daniel together — praising God every step of the way!

In Christ,
David Wayne Meeker

"Behold, I am with you always, even to the end of the age."

— Jesus Christ in Matthew 24:20

"30At that time the sign of the Son of Man will appear in heaven, and all the tribes of the earth will mourn. They will see the Son of Man coming on the clouds of heaven, with power and great glory. 31And He will send out His angels with a loud trumpet call, and they will gather His elect from the four winds, from one end of the heavens to the other."

— Jesus Christ in Matthew 24:30-31

The 70th-Week of Daniel's Chronological Order

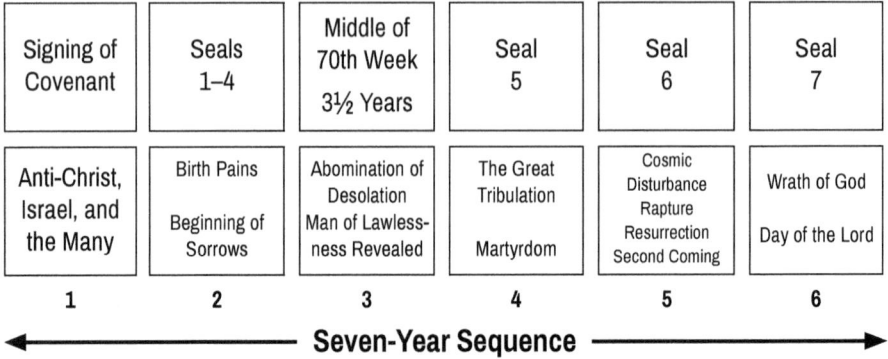

Signing of Covenant	Seals 1–4	Middle of 70th Week 3½ Years	Seal 5	Seal 6	Seal 7
Anti-Christ, Israel, and the Many	Birth Pains Beginning of Sorrows	Abomination of Desolation Man of Lawlessness Revealed	The Great Tribulation Martyrdom	Cosmic Disturbance Rapture Resurrection Second Coming	Wrath of God Day of the Lord
1	2	3	4	5	6

◄——————— Seven-Year Sequence ———————►

The chronological chart above represents the information found in passage parallels from The Book of Daniel, The Book of Joel, The Book of Matthew, The Book of Luke, The Book of Mark, 1 Corinthians, 1 and 2 Thessalonians, and The Book of Revelation. Displaying the chronological order of The 70th Week of Daniel's information, along with its passage parallels in a chart format, can help us to visually understand these passage-parallel prophecies in their proper chronological sequences more fully. Below I have a chart showing the sequence of the seven Seals, the seven Trumpets, and the seven Bowls.

Beginning of Sorrows: Seals 1-4

The 70th Week of Daniel is really a series of catastrophic events caused by man and Satan — allowed by God — which are identified as seven Seals in the Book of Revelation and has begun with the signing of the covenant between the anti-Christ, the Nation of Israel, and the many (Da. 9:27). The anti-Christ's identity is not known here at the beginning (Rev. 6:1-2; 2Th. 2:4). The Beginning of Sorrows (i.e. Birth Pains), involves the first four Seals of The Book of Revelation (Rev. 5; 6:1-17; 8:1-6) and includes the following:

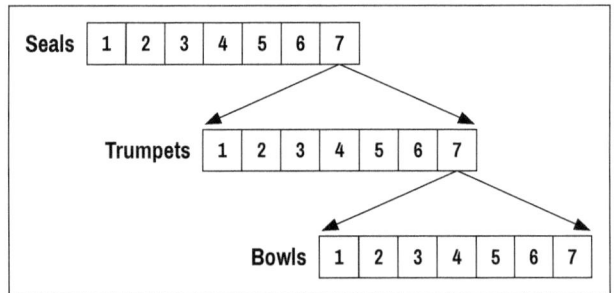

1.) The *first Seal* which introduced a peaceful conqueror, the anti-Christ, who at this time is not known as the anti-Christ — onto the scene as a rider on a White Horse who wears a crown and carries a bow, but John does not mention that he has arrows (Rev. 6:1-2). Many Bible scholars believe that is because he will conquer without using a sword, but through diplomacy, and will deceive many with talks of peace, but he will wage war against the elect, both Jews and Christians (Da. 12:1; Mt. 24:21-22; Rev. 6:9-11; 12:17); despite the promise of peace from the anti-Christ, intense wars are occurring and will occur on Earth at this time; **2.) The *second Seal***, during which the rider on the Red Horse slays a great number of people and will take the peace from Earth away — which could be a possible description of international and/or many civil wars (Rev. 6:3-4); **3.) The *third Seal*** in which the rider on the Black Horse will spread famine throughout the earth possibly as a consequence of wars, or food production shortages, or possibly the result of inflation like we are experiencing now in 2023, but much worse, which causes a financial and famine crisis globally (Rev. 6:5-6), or all the above possible causes combined; and **4.) The *fourth Seal***, Death, described as a rider on a Pale Horse having power over one-quarter of the earth to kill with a sword and through more plagues that could be, according to some Bible scholars, similar to a bubonic plague, famine, pestilence, earthquakes, more war, and death by wild beasts on the earth (Rev. 6:7-8; Mt. 24:7; Mk. 13:8). Many Bible scholars have attributed one-quarter of the deaths of the world's population to the first through fourth Seals as accumulated from the great wars, famines, bubonic and other plagues, and pestilence—either man-made, natural, or supernatural. These present sufferings of the elect are not worth comparing to what is in store for us in Heaven (1Cor. 2:9; Ro. 8:18-19).

The Building of the Jewish Temple in Jerusalem

Sometime between the first Seal and the fifth Seal, probably closer to the second Seal, is when the long-awaited Jewish Temple will be built.[1] It will not be a magnificent, gold-layered Temple like Solomon's Temple was. The

---

1   The Temple Institute of Israel purchased five (5) red heifers on September 10, 2022 to be used in its temple purification ceremonies as prescribed in Scripture. As of 2023, the red heifers are approximately one and a half to two years old, and, according to Scripture, cannot be used until they are at least three years old (Ge. 15:9; Num. 19:1-22). http://templeinstitute.org/red-heifer/

Bible tells us it will be built, but in times of trouble, with streets and a trench (Da. 9:25). It could even be built quickly and simply and could be similar to a tabernacle; but one thing we can be sure of is that it will be built, because the Bible tells us that the Third Temple will be defiled by the anti-Christ 3-½ years after the start of Daniel's 70th Week (Da. 9:27; Mt. 24:15; 2Th. 2:1-12). See the chart below.

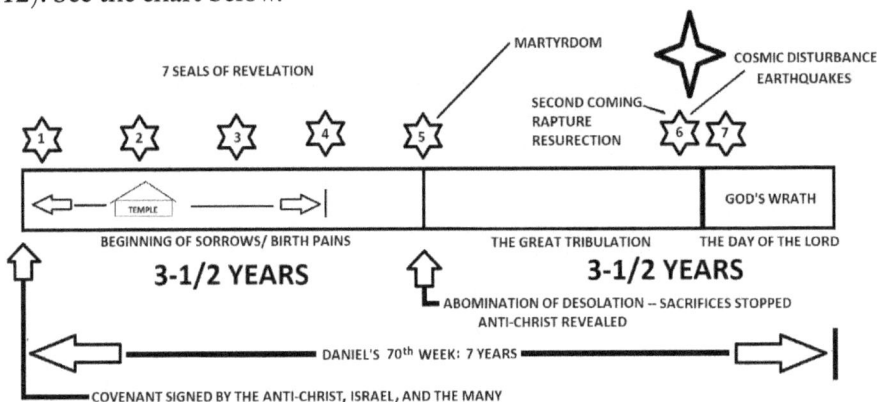

Midpoint: 3-½ Years

At the midpoint of Daniel's 70th Week, the man of lawlessness is revealed at the moment of the abomination of desolation (Da. 9:27; 2Th. 2:4) when he sits in the Temple and declares himself as God (Mt. 24:15; 2Th. 2:3-4). The man of lawlessness will be revealed at that time and will perform demonic signs and false wonders and deceive many people (2Th. 2:9-10). Jesus will overthrow the man of lawlessness at His Second Coming "...with the breath of His mouth and destroy him by the splendor of His coming" (2Th. 2:8; Rev. 19:19-21). Hallelujah!

The Great Tribulation: Begins at the Fifth Seal

The fifth Seal speaks of the deaths of the elect, both Jew and Christian (Rev. 6:9-11). The events of The Great Tribulation occur after the abomination of desolation at the 3½-year midpoint of Daniel's 70th Week and will include persecution and martyrdom (Mt. 24:9; Rev. 6:9; 13:7), apostasy (Mt. 24:10, 12; 2Th. 2:3), false prophets (Mt. 24:11; Rev. 19:20), and many people being deceived (Mt. 24:11, 24; 2Th. 2:9-10; Rev. 13:14; 19:20). They will be deceived by lying signs and wonders (Mt. 24:24; 2Th. 2:9; Rev. 13:13-14; 19:20). There will be an increase of wickedness (Mt. 24:12; 2Th. 2:7; Rev. 13:8). The Two Witnesses will begin their ministry (Rev. 11:3).

The Cosmic Disturbance & Its Purpose: The Sixth Seal

The sixth Seal includes the Cosmic Disturbance (i.e. catastrophic events) — massive earthquakes (Rev. 6:12-14; Mk. 13:24-27), the sun turning black, the moon turning blood red, stars falling from the sky, and mountains and islands disappearing (Rev. 6:12-14), The Second Coming of Jesus Christ — with every eye seeing Him (Mt. 24:30-31; 1Th. 4:16-18; Rev. 1:7), the Bodily Resurrection (Jn. 5:28-29; 1Cor. 15:51-53; 1Th. 4:13-18; Ph. 3:20-21), and the Rapture (1Cor. 15:50-54; 1Th. 4:16-17; 1Th. 5:1-8; Rev. 3:10). Then the elect (Lk. 10:20) will be judged by Jesus Christ (2Cor. 5:10) and then go to a place Christ has prepared for us (Jn. 14:3). I want to point out that the Cosmic Disturbance has two main functions: 1.) it will shorten the Great Tribulation for the sake of the elect, and 2.) it will also announce the beginning of the Day of the Lord (Is. 13:9-11; Joel 2:10, 30-31; Mt. 24:29; Mk. 13:24-27; Lk. 21:25-28; Rev. 6:12-14). Before the start of the seventh Seal, the 144,000 Jews from the twelve tribes of Israel are sealed by God for protection (Rev.7:3-8). Elijah will come prior to the seventh Seal (Mic. 4:5-6). Elijah could be one of the Two Witnesses (Rev. 11:3-12).

The Day of the Lord: The Contents of the Seventh Seal

The seventh Seal contains the Day of the Lord and God's Judgments (Rev. 6:17; 2Pe. 3:10) and silence in heaven for half an hour (Rev. 8:1), and includes the seven Trumpets (Rev. 8:1-5), and the seven Bowls of God's Wrath.

The Seven Trumpets

The seven Trumpets include the following: 1.) the First Trumpet: hailstones and fire destroy one-third of all plant life (Rev. 8:7), 2.) the Second Trumpet: a third of the sea turns to blood and destroys one-third of all sea life (Rev. 8:8-9), 3.) the Third Trumpet: destroys a third of all the rivers and the spring water supply (Rev. 8:10-11). 4.) the Fourth Trumpet: one-third of the moon, stars, and sun darkens (Rev. 8:12), 5.) the Fifth Trumpet: locusts torture people for five months, and those who are stung will wish for death (Rev. 9:3-11), 6.) the Sixth Trumpet: four fallen angels are released and wipe out people with sulfur and fire, and they kill a third of all the people on Earth (Rev. 9:12-21), and 7.) the Seventh Trumpet: Seven angels have the Seven Bowls of God's Wrath (Rev. 11:15-19), and the Two Witnesses are killed (Rev. 11:7).

The Seven Bowls

The Seven Bowls include the following: 1.) painful sores on humans (Rev. 16:2), 2.) death of everything in the sea (Rev.16:3), 3.) rivers turning to blood (Rev.16:4), 4.) the sun causing great pain (Rev. 16:8-9), 5.) great darkness and worsened sores from the First Bowl (Rev. 16:10-11), 6.) the Euphrates River drying up and the anti-Christ's armies gathering for Armageddon (Rev. 16:12-16), and 7.) a great earthquake and a giant hailstorm (Rev. 16:17-21). The resurrection of the Two Witnesses will also occur during this time (Rev. 11:11).

The Elect Will Overcome

The Bible uses the term *overcoming* in slightly two different ways: 1.) Christians will *overcome* the anti-Christ by loving Jesus more than their own lives, which is an eternal, spiritual victory for the elect (Rev. 12:11), and 2.) the anti-Christ shall overcome Christians by persecuting and killing them, which is a temporary, physical victory for the anti-Christ (Rev. 13:7) — but is also, at the same time, an eternal, spiritual victory for the elect (Rev. 12:11). The anti-Christ just can't win (Mt. 10:29; Ph. 1:21; Rev. 20:2-5).

Below, I want again to show you a chronological chart that attempts to represent all the information found in passage parallels from The Book of Daniel, The Book of Joel, The Book of Matthew, The Book of Luke, the Book of Mark, First Corinthians, 1 and 2 Thessalonians, and The Book of Revelation, and many other books and passages. As I display the chronological order of the information of The 70th Week of Daniel, along with its passage-parallels content in a chart format, I believe that this format will help us to visually understand these passage-parallels prophecies in their proper chronological sequences more fully. Below, we will look at the *Pre-Wrath Creed* that also takes the same parallel passages, plus many other passages throughout Scripture to create a broader context of the Word of God as a whole, and communicates them in a concise, vernacular format to help us better understand this prophetic information more thoroughly.

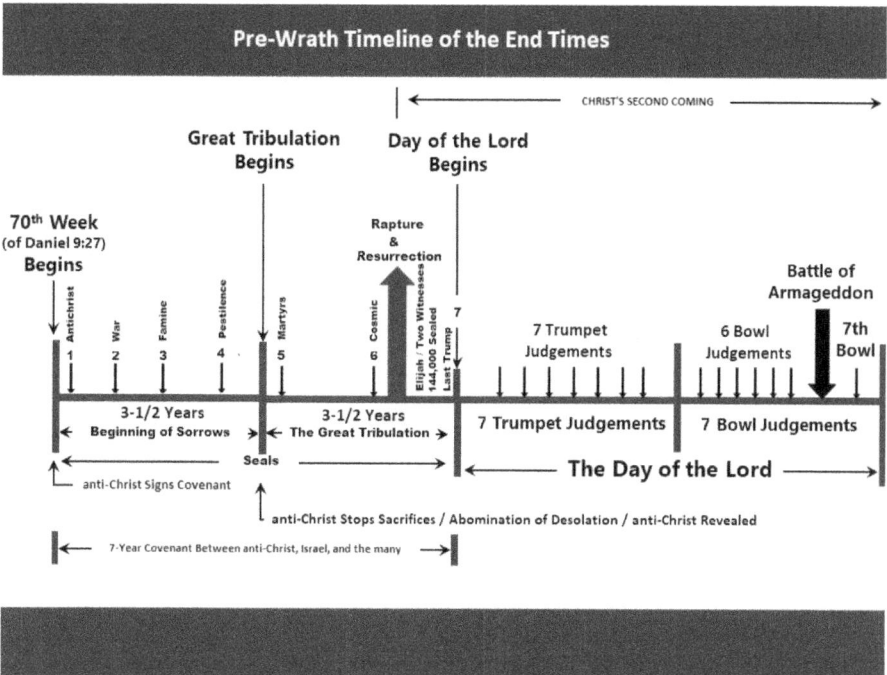

The Pre-Wrath Creed

We believe the Bible is the inspired Word of God and is profitable for doctrine, for reproof, for correction, for instruction in righteousness (2Ti. 3:16). We believe the Bible is true (Ps. 33:24), perfect (Ps. 18:30), and the sole source of all truth pertaining to the personal attributes, characteristics of God, the condition of man (Is. 64:6), and His plan of redemption (Ro. 5:9). We believe the Bible should be studied (2Ti. 2:15), obeyed (1Jn. 2:3), and shared (1Pe. 3:15). We believe God is eternal (Ps. 45:6), God is Love, (1Jn. 4:8), God is Spirit (Jn. 4:24), God is One (Is. 46:9; Gal. 3:20), and God cannot lie (Tit. 1:2). We believe God knows all things (Ps. 147:9). We believe God is the Creator and Sustainer of the universe (Is. 40:28; Heb. 1:3). We believe God created man in His own image (Ge. 1:27). We believe God created the Earth, solar system, and everything in it (Col. 1:16) in six literal days (Ge. 1:31) and rested on the 7th day (Ge. 2:2). We believe sin originated in Heaven by an angel named Lucifer and he was cast down to Earth (Is. 14:12-15). We believe sin and death entered the world through Adam's disobedience (Ge. 3:1, 6; Ro. 5:19). We believe through his disobedience, sin and death passed on to all people (Ro. 5:12). We believe there is one God revealed in Three Persons — the Father, Son, and Holy Spirit (Mt. 3:16-17; 1Pe. 1:2). We believe Jesus Christ is the Son of God (1Jn. 4:15) and the Second Person of the Trinity (1Jn. 5:7), being the eternal God and equal in substance (Col. 2:9) to the Father and Holy Spirit and took upon Himself the nature of a man (Phil. 2:8) with all the essential properties and common infirmities but without sin (2Co. 5:21). We believe He was conceived by the Holy Spirit (Mt. 1:18) and born of a virgin (Lk. 1:27), being fully God and fully man with two whole perfect and distinct natures, the Godhead and manhood (Col. 2:9). We believe Jesus was sent by God the Father as our Sacrifice (Jn. 3:16) and Savior (Jn. 3:17; 2Th. 1:8,9) from everlasting punishment (Mt. 25:48) in Hell (Mt. 25:41; Ro. 6:23). We believe Jesus Christ suffered (1Pe. 4:1) and died on a cross and was buried and rose again on the third day bodily and appeared to over five hundred witnesses (1Cor. 15:2-6). We believe Jesus ascended to Heaven and sits at the right hand of the Father (Mk. 16:19) and will return in the same manner He ascended (Ac. 1:10, 11). We believe the wicked occupants of Earth will be righteously judged by their Creator God at the End of the Age (Ge. 1:1; Ps. 96:13; Is. 33:22; 2Ti. 4:1). We believe the future time prophesied by Daniel in his 70th Week will begin at the signing of a covenant between the anti-Christ, the Nation of Israel, and the many (Da. 9:27). We believe the 70th Week of Daniel will last seven years prior to the end of current human history at the End of the Age (Da. 8:13-14). We believe the combined information found within Daniel's 70th week, Jesus' teaching found in His Olivet Discourse (Mt. 24:1-25:46), and the prophecies made by the Apostle John in the Book of Revelation (Rev. 5-8), with regard to the Scroll and the seven Seals, are harmonious and consistent in their content, and together describe in detail the worst events known, or that ever will be known, in human history on Earth (Mt. 24:21; Da. 12:1; Rev. 7:14). We believe Jesus taught His disciples that no one knows the day or the hour of His Second Coming and the End of the Age, except His Father (Mt. 24:36). We believe Jesus taught His disciples that they would know and understand the season, and to be alert and be watchful (Mt. 24:3-7; Mk. 13:32-33; Lk. 21:25-28). We believe that believers are exhorted to keep watch and be ready for Christ's return (Mt. 24:42-44; 1Th. 5:4-6). We believe Jesus taught His disciples many details about the events that will occur prior to His Second Coming and the End of the Age (Mt. 24:3-31; 2Ti. 3:1-5). We believe Jesus told His disciples many details with regard to the signs that would be present at the time leading up to His Second Coming, such as religious deceptions and many false Christ's (Mt. 25:5), wars and rumors of wars (Mt. 24:6; Rev. 6:3-4), famines and earthquakes (Mt. 24:7; Rev. 6:7-8), death and martyrdom (Mt. 24:21-22; Rev. 6:9-11; 12:17), economic crisis (Rev. 6:5-6), and pestilences (Mt. 24:5-7; Mk. 13:8; Rev. 6:7-8). We believe Christ taught His disciples there would be an increase in the intensity of these signs leading up to His Second Coming and described these events as Birth Pains (Mt. 24:8). We believe Birth Pains and the Great Tribulation are the result of both the wrath of Satan and man (Rev. 12:12, 17). We believe Satan was given permission by God for 3½ years to persecute and kill both Jews and Christians (Job 1:1-22; Rev. 13:5, 7). We believe because of the anti-Christ's hatred for both Jews and Christians that he will most likely be a Muslim (Da. 7-8; 11:32-45). We believe the Muslim anti-Christ will change the appointed times to an Islamic calendar or hijri, which is a lunar calendar. We believe the anti-Christ will change the laws to Islamic laws, Quran and Sunnah, which make up Shariah law (Da. 7:25). We believe the anti-Christ and the false prophet will receive power and authority from Satan (2Cor. 4:4). We believe Satan, the anti-Christ, and the false prophet are an unholy trinity (Rev. 20:10). We believe the content of the Scroll, not the Seals themselves, is the Wrath of God. We believe the rider of the white horse that we read about in Rev. 6:1-2 carries a bow, but has no arrows, symbolizes a bloodless victory, and represents a victory that is accomplished through peaceful negotiations and diplomacy, rather than conquering with war and a sword. We believe the rider on a white horse mentioned in Rev. 6:1-2 is not the same as the Rider on a white horse that we read about in Rev. 19:11-16. We believe the rider of the white horse in Rev. 6:1-2 is the anti-Christ, and the Rider on the white horse in Rev. 19:11-16 is Jesus Christ. We believe the signs prior to Christ's Second Coming and the End of the Age will include many false Christ's and false prophets that will arise and deceive many (Mt. 24:24), including both Jews and Christians (Mt. 24:10, 12; 2Th. 2:3). We believe the anti-Christ will require all the people in the world to receive a mark on their right hand or forehead in order to buy and sell (Rev. 13:11-18). We believe that during The 70th Week of Daniel lawlessness will abound (Mt. 24:12-13). We believe the Gospel will be preached to all the Nations, and then the end will come (Mt. 24:14). We believe the Birth Pains and the Beginning of Sorrows are synonymous with the first four Seals (Da. 9; Rev 6:1-8; Mt. 24:8-13), mentioned by Jesus, the Prophet Daniel, and the Apostle John, and will start when the anti-Christ makes a covenant with Israel and the many, as mentioned by the Prophet Daniel (Da. 9:27). We believe Jesus will come to Earth a total of two times, as Scripture has clearly indicated, and when Christ comes the second time, His coming will be physical and visible — just as His first coming (Is. 9:6-7; Mt. 1:18-25; Mt. 24:30-31; 1Th. 4:16-17; Rev. 1:7). We believe the teaching that Christ will come three times — once invisible and twice visible — is not Biblically justified or substantiated (Heb. 9:28). We believe Christ will return in the same way He ascended (Ac. 1:10-11). We believe when Christ returns at His Second Coming that no one will know the day or the hour (Mt. 24:36), but we will know the season (Mt. 24) and every eye will see Him (Rev. 1:7). We believe Jesus mentioned the Prophet Daniel in His Olivet Discourse, and referred to the seven-year covenant (Da. 9:27; Mt. 24:1-40) and the Abomination of Desolation (Da. 9:27; Mt. 24:15). We believe that Christ and the prophet Daniel believed there would be a literal Temple built sometime during the beginning of the first half of The 70th Week of Daniel during the Beginning of Sorrows and/or Birth Pains (Da. 9:24-27; Mt. 24:15). We believe the anti-Christ will sit in the Temple and declare himself

God (Mt. 24:15; 1Th. 2:3-4). We believe the reference by Christ to the Prophet Daniel's 70th Week establishes a specific timeline of the Second Coming of Jesus Christ and the End of the Age. We believe the Abomination of Desolation will occur at the midpoint of Daniel's 70th Week (Da. 9:26-27; Mt. 24:15). We believe that at the moment the anti-Christ commits the Abomination of Desolation, the anti-Christ will be revealed (Da. 9:27; 2Th. 2:4-8). We believe there will be many false Christ's and false prophets at the End of the Age (Mt. 24:11, 24; Rev. 19:20). We believe people of every nation will be deceived and worship the anti-Christ (Mt. 24:11, 24; 2 Th. 2:9-10; Rev. 13:14, 19:20). We believe the anti-Christ will deceive many by using lying signs and wonders received by Satan (Mt. 24:24; 2Th. 2:9-12; Rev. 13:13-14, 19:20). We believe all the non-believing world will be caught unaware at Jesus' Second Coming (Mt. 24:39; 1Th. 5:3). We believe those who disbelieve God's truth and delight in wickedness will receive a powerful delusion by God to believe the lie (2Th. 2:10-12). We believe when Jesus returns, He will be like a thief in the night to the non-believing people of the world, and they will be unprepared (Mt. 24:43-50; 1Th. 5:2, 4). We believe a religious apostasy will occur (Mt. 24:10, 12; 2Th. 2:3; Rev. 3:16). We believe during Daniel's 70th Week there will be an increase of wickedness (Mt. 24:12; 2Th. 2:7-8; Rev. 13:8). We believe when the people of the world say "peace and security," sudden destruction will come upon them, and they will not escape (1Th. 5:3). We believe the restraining force that protects Israel (2Th. 2:7) is the angelic "prince," Michael the Archangel (Da. 10:20-21; 12:1; Rev. 12:7-9). We believe God will allow the restraining force (i.e. the archangel Michael) to arise and move out of the way prior to the anti-Christ's proclaiming to be God and the anti-Christ's sitting in the Temple at the beginning of the Great Tribulation at the midpoint of Daniel's 70th week (Da. 12:1; Mt. 24: 15; 2Th. 2:3-4; 6-9). We believe that after the restraining force is taken out of the way, the anti-Christ (i.e. the lawless one) will be revealed (2Th. 2:7-8). We believe the restrainer (i.e. the archangel Michael) will be removed prior to the Abomination of Desolation at the 3½-year midpoint of Daniel's 70th week (Mt. 24:15; 2Th. 2:7-8). We believe all the people of every nation whose name is not written in the Book of Life will worship the anti-Christ

(Rev. 13:7-8). We believe the anti-Christ will demand to be worshipped by the world, and those who refuse will be hunted down and killed for God's name's sake (Mt. 24:9; Rev. 6:9; 12:17; 13:7, 15). We believe Jesus Christ will annihilate the anti-Christ by His majesty at His arrival (2Th. 2:8). We believe Daniel's 70th Week (Da. 9:24-27) is a key to understanding the timing of the Second Coming of Christ and the End of the Age, together with the Olivet Discourse Prophecies and the Apostle John's Book of Revelation and the Scroll and seven Seals (Rev. 6-8). We believe the Beginning of Birth Pains (i.e. the Beginning of Sorrows) of Jesus' Olivet Discourse (Mt. 24:8) correspond perfectly with the Seals found in the Book of Revelation (Rev. 5-8). We believe the first five Seals that are wrapped around the Scroll are the wrath of Satan and man (Mt. 24:3-7; Rev. 12:12-17). We Believe the Cosmic Disturbance at the sixth Seal is the event that cuts short the Great Tribulation for the sake of the elect (Mt. 24:21-22). We believe the seventh Seal is the Day of the Lord (Rev. 8:1-5). We believe when the seventh Seal is opened, there will be silence in Heaven for about thirty minutes (Rev. 8:1). We believe the content inside the Scroll is actually the Wrath of God, which includes the seven Trumpets and seven Bowl Judgments (Rev. 8:1-6). We believe The Battle of Armageddon will start after the seven Bowl Judgments (Rev. 19:1-19). We believe the Beginnings of Sorrows (Birth Pains) will begin with the signing of a seven-year covenant between the anti-Christ, the Nation of Israel, and the many (Da. 9:27; Isa 28:15). We believe the anti-Christ will allow Israel to begin sacrifices and grain offerings, but will cut off this agreement after 3½ years (Da. 11:31; 12:11). We believe that at the time of the Abomination of Desolation, the anti-Christ will be revealed and demand the world worship him as God in the new Temple (Mt. 24:15; Da. 11:31). We believe many of the Jews and the Christians will refuse to worship the anti-Christ and will be sought out and martyred (Rev. 6:9-11). We believe the fifth Seal in Revelation (Rev. 6:9-11) corresponds perfectly with the teachings of Jesus' Olivet Discourse (Mt. 24:21-22; Rev. 12:17). We believe the Cosmic Disturbance mentioned by the Apostle John (Rev. 6:12-17) corresponds perfectly with Jesus' Olivet Discourse in (Mt. 24:29) and both Joel 2:28-32 and Acts 2:20. We believe the Cosmic Disturbance will occur at the sixth Seal, as indicated in the Book of Revelation (Rev. 6:12-17). We believe the Rapture of the Church will occur immediately prior to the beginning of The Day of the Lord (Rev. 8:1-6). We believe The Day of the Lord commences sometime within the second half of the 70th Week after the sixth Seal (Mt. 24:29; Rev. 6:12-17). We believe the Cosmic Disturbance associated with the sixth Seal will signal the beginning of the Day of the Lord. We believe The Day of the Lord will begin at the opening of the seventh Seal (Rev. 8:1). We believe the Day of the Lord is coming with cruel fury and burning anger — to make Earth a desolation and to destroy the sinners within it (Is. 13:9). We believe God will punish the world for its evil, and the wicked for their iniquity (Is. 13:11). We believe the Cosmic Disturbance will occur before the Day of the Lord and after the Great Tribulation, as indicated in Scripture (Mt. 24:29-30; Rev. 6:12-17; Joel 2:31). We believe that after the Cosmic Disturbance occurs, the Son of Man will come in the clouds with Great Power and Glory to gather His elect (Mk. 13:24, 33; Lk. 21:25-28). We believe the Bodily Resurrection of the elect and the Second Coming of Christ will simultaneously occur and every eye will see Him; and Christ's coming will be loud, noisy, and visible — not silent and invisible (Mt. 24:30-31; Rev. 1:7). We believe the Second Coming of Christ, the Rapture, and the Resurrection will occur immediately before the opening of the seventh Seal and after the Cosmic Disturbance (1Th. 4:16-17). We believe Elijah must appear before the Day of the Lord (Mal. 4:5-6). We believe there will be Two Witnesses that will arrive and preach for 3½ years at the second half of Daniel's 70th Week, beginning at the Great Tribulation, wearing sackcloth, and performing signs and wonders (Rev. 11:3). We believe the Two Witnesses will be killed and lay dead in the street for 3½ days (Rev. 11:7). We believe the Two Witnesses will be resurrected from the dead after 3½ days (1Cor. 15:51-52; 1Th. 4:17; Rev. 11:11). We believe The Day of the Lord is synonymous with The Day of God's Wrath (Is.13:9, 11; Zep. 1:14-18). We believe that before the seventh Seal, the 144,000 will be sealed for protection by God (Rev. 7:3-8). We believe the great multitude in Heaven mentioned in the Book of Revelation are the martyrs from the Great Tribulation as indicated by Scripture (Rev. 6:9-17). We believe that before the seventh Seal, the Last Trumpet will be blown

(1Cor. 15:51-52; 1Th.4:16-17). We believe the Last Trumpet in this context signifies a call to gather the elect at Christ's Second Coming (Num. 10:1-36; 1Cor. 15:52; 1Th. 4:16). We believe the last Trumpet in 1 Thessalonians is not the same Trumpet as in the Book of Revelation. We believe that before the seventh Seal, the Apostasy will occur (Mt. 24:10, 12; 2Th. 2:3) and the man of sin will be revealed (Da. 9:27; 2Th. 2:4). We believe the man of sin will be revealed at the Abomination of Desolation. We believe once the seven Seals are broken, then the Wrath of God will commence and there will be silence in heaven for about half an hour (Rev. 8:1-6). We believe the Millennial Reign of Christ will begin after the Battle of Armageddon (Rev. 16:12-16; 19:11-20). We believe the Battle of Armageddon is synonymous with the sixth Bowl Judgment and will occur at Christ's Second Coming (Rev. 16:12-16). We believe Jesus will judge both the living and the dead (Jn. 5:22; Ac. 10:42). We believe Jesus Christ is the only mediator between God and people (1Ti. 2:5). We believe salvation is a gift from God (Eph. 2:8, 9; 1Jn. 5:11, 12) and a Work of the Holy Spirit (Jn. 16:8-11) and comes by grace through faith in Jesus Christ (Col. 1:14; Ro. 3:24) as we repent of our sin (Lk. 13:3; Mk. 1:15) and abide in Christ (2Jn. 1:9). We believe baptism symbolizes the death, burial, and resurrection of our Lord Jesus Christ (Col. 2:12) and is important but not necessary for salvation (Mk. 16:16; Lk. 23:43; Lk. 7:50). We believe a new believer should be baptized as an act of obedience (Ac. 2:38). We believe the sacrifice of Christ alone was and is sufficient for our sin (Eph. 2:8, 9; 2Cor. 5:21; 1Jn. 1:7). We believe we need God to know God (Jn. 6:44; 1Cor. 2:14). We believe a change occurs in the heart of a person who comes to Christ (Ro. 12:2; 2Cor. 5:17), and at the point of this conversion and forward, their desires and motives will habitually glorify God and not themselves (Jn. 3:30; 2 Cor. 1:12). We believe faith is dead without works (Ja. 2:17). We believe a disciple will always struggle with sin in this life (Ro. 7:15-25) but is justified (Ac. 13:39), sanctified (Heb. 10:10), and has no condemnation in Christ (Ro. 8:1). We believe a disciple will obey God (Jn. 14:15; Jn. 10:27), pray to God (Eph. 6:18), worship God (Ex 34:14), and praise God (Ps. 150:1-6). We believe a disciple will abide in Christ (Jn. 15:4-8; Col. 2:6), practice righteousness (1Jn. 3:7), remain pure (1Jn. 5:18), not habitually sin (1Jn. 3:9; Ro. 6:1), and overcome the world (1Jn. 4:4; 5:5). We believe a disciple will share the Gospel (Eph. 3:8), make other disciples and baptize them (Mt. 28:19), and teach them the commands of Christ (Mt. 28:20). We believe "today is the day of salvation" (2Cor. 6:2). We believe a disciple will love his or her neighbor (Mt. 22:39), love other disciples (Jn. 13:34, 35), and will fellowship with believers in love and unity (Heb. 10:25). We believe disciples will deny themselves, carry their cross, and follow Jesus (Mt. 16:24). We believe disciples will love God with all their heart, mind, soul, and strength (Mk. 12:30), rightly divide the Word of Truth (2Ti. 2:15) and will be ready to give an answer for the hope that is in them with gentleness and respect (1Pe. 3:15), be fruitful (Jn. 15:5-8), and evangelize (Mt. 28:18-20). We believe as disciples we need to fight the good fight, finish the race, and keep the faith (2Ti. 4:7); and submit to (Jam. 4:7), surrender to (1Pe. 5:7), serve (Col. 3:24), and obey (Lk. 11:28) God. We believe God's grace, mercy, peace, truth, and love abide in us (2Jn. 1:2, 3). We believe that at the moment of our physical death, we will be in the presence of the Lord (2 Cor. 5:8), judged (Heb. 9:27) and found innocent through the blood of Christ (Jn. 10:28; Rev. 1:5), and we will live a new life in eternity (Ro. 6:23; Jn. 3:16) with God (Rev. 22:3,4) in a new Heaven and new Earth (Is. 65:17; 66:22; 1Cor. 2:9; Rev. 21:1-27; 22:34). Amen!

The Four Major Views

DETERMINING AN ACCURATE BIBLICAL VIEW
THROUGH HERMENEUTICS

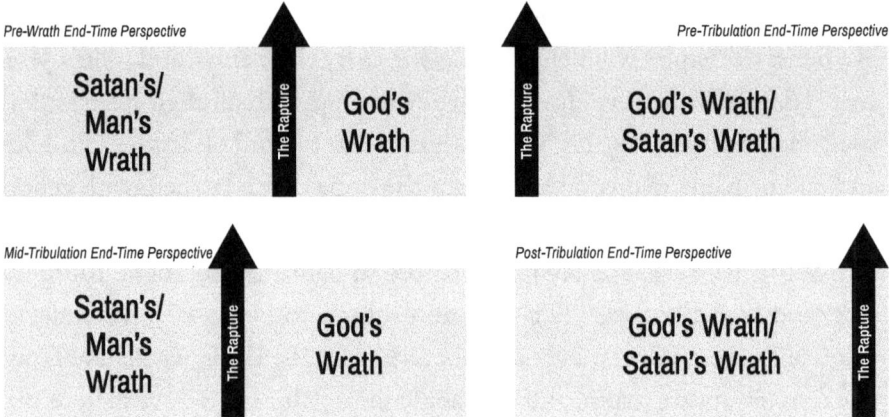

Pre-Wrath End-Time Perspective

Satan's/ Man's Wrath	The Rapture	God's Wrath

Pre-Tribulation End-Time Perspective

The Rapture	God's Wrath/ Satan's Wrath

Mid-Tribulation End-Time Perspective

Satan's/ Man's Wrath	The Rapture	God's Wrath

Post-Tribulation End-Time Perspective

God's Wrath/ Satan's Wrath	The Rapture

Chapter 1

Fundamentals of Understanding: Terminology

I want to point out some crucially important issues which are fundamental to the correct understanding of the events of the End Time. The Bible certainly reveals to us that there will come a traumatic seven-year period of time in the future where God will bring history to both an appropriate and righteous conclusion. I want to mention how critically important it is that we refer to the future seven-year tribulation period by its proper Biblical name: The 70th Week of the Book of Daniel. This future period of time is frequently but inaccurately referred to as the Tribulation Period. I think that this inaccurate interpretation can lead to a misunderstanding of the timing of the Rapture and events related to Christ's Second Coming. In other words, the term Tribulation Period and how it has been used has been consistently used to refer to the future seven-year period of Daniel's 70th Week without any Biblical justification. We must remember that the Holy Bible teaches that the elect will not experience the Wrath of God but does not promise protection from the wrath of Satan and man. In the Book of Revelation 13:5, 7 — permission is given to the anti-Christ to persecute and kill the Saints for 3-½ years, similarly to when God gave permission to Satan to persecute Job (Job 1). This is precisely at the second half of Daniel's 70th Week, identified as the beginning of the Great Tribulation, or the midpoint of Daniel's 70th Week. Three-and-one-half years into Daniels 70th Week, the anti-Christ is revealed when the Abomination of Desolation occurs (Da. 9:7; Mt. 24:15;

Mk. 13:14). It is at this point that the anti-Christ is given permission to kill the saints for 3½ years by God (Rev. 13:5, 7), which means that the 70th Week of Daniel is not an expression of God's Wrath but is an expression of man's and Satan's wrath. The killing of the elect, both Jews and Christians, will start at the midpoint, or the 3½-year mark, of Daniel's 70th Week, after the Abomination of Desolation occurs (Mt. 24:15; Da. 9:27). At that time, the anti-Christ will demand to be worshiped as God in the Jewish Temple (2Th. 2:4). When Jews and Christians refuse to worship the anti-Christ, he will begin killing all those who refuse to worship him through beheading (Rev. 20:4). God's Wrath does not begin until after Jesus comes for His elect (1Th. 1:10), at the sixth Seal (Rev. 6:12).

Revelation 13:5-7:

> *"⁵The beast was given a mouth to speak arrogant and blasphemous words, and authority to act for forty-two months. ⁶And the beast opened its mouth to blaspheme against God and slander His name and His tabernacle—those who dwell in heaven. ⁷Then the beast was permitted to wage war against the saints and conquer them, and it was given authority over every tribe and people and tongue and nation. ⁸And all who dwell on the earth will worship the beast—all whose names have not been written from the foundation of the world in the book of life of the Lamb who was slain."*

The correct answers to these questions regarding the End Times are fundamentally important in getting a proper understanding for the timing of the Rapture and Resurrection of the elect, and Christ's Second Coming. I will give you solid answers to these questions found only in God's Word that positively identify the beginning of Daniel's 70th Week — at the signing of a covenant between the anti-Christ, the Nation of Israel, and the many, which parallels perfectly with Jesus' Olivet Discourse in Matthew 24 and John's Book of Revelation 5-8. Most Bible-believing Christians agree that true believers (i.e. the elect) are not subject to God's Wrath. This promise found in Scripture was penned by the Apostle Paul, as he was moved by the Holy Spirit, and assures us that God will not subject believers to His Judgments when He pours out His wrath upon a rebellious world (1Th. 5:9). I want to point out to you that the misunderstanding of the proper usage of Biblical terminology can lead to some un-Biblical assumptions. Case-in-Point: if you refer to The 70th Week of Daniel by its incorrect name –the Tribulation Period — it will be easier for you to reason that all seven years of the so-called Tribulation Period are caused by God and, therefore, must represent the Wrath of God. This flawed reasoning results in the faulty conclusion that Christians must experience the Rapture prior to the so-called Tribulation Period, which means that the Rapture would have to occur prior to the final seven-year so-called Tribulation Period because of the Biblical teaching that Christians will not be subject to God's Wrath. The Pre-Tribulation, Mid-Tribulation, and the Post-Tribulation views currently are the most popular views held by many faithful church congregations and Godly Christians today, even though these views cannot be fully substantiated or fully justified with Scripture. The Old Testament Prophets, the Lord Jesus Christ Himself, the Apostle John, and the Prophet Daniel all definitely taught that God's Wrath will not begin until well inside the final seven-year period of time and that it will become significantly less than seven years, because God will cut The Great Tribulation short for the sake of the elect through a Cosmic Disturbance. I believe this misunderstanding occurred when believers began to interpret Daniel's Beginnings of Sorrows and The Great Tribulation all as the Tribulation Period and started using the words *"The Tribulation"* as synonymous with the Beginning of Sorrows and The Great Tribulation. There is a difference between the words *"The Tribulation"* and the term "The Great Tribulation" and they are not one-and-the-same or interchangeable. God promises that the elect will not be subjected to His Wrath, but He does not promise that the elect will not be subject to Satan's and man's wrath. The wrath of Satan and man has been occurring on earth throughout all of history, since the fall of man in the Garden. Also, I want to point out that the Pre-Wrath position is really not a new position within the Church at all. The only thing that is new about the Pre-Wrath position is the name itself. The view that the Church would see the anti-Christ and be removed prior to God's Judgments was, without question, the view of the early Church fathers.

The Pre-Wrath Rapture view, I believe, is the correct view, and I will show you — through Scripture — why I believe that the Pre-Wrath Rapture view aligns better than any other Rapture view mentioned in this book. Because of the significance of this particular truth, and at the risk of being redundant, I want to mention to you again that the Bible does not refer to all of the seven years of Daniel's 70th Week as the Tribulation Period anywhere in the Bible. The first 3-½ years of Daniel's 70th Week is referred to as the Beginning of Sorrows (i.e. Birth Pains). The last 3 ½ years is referred to as The Great Tribulation. Jesus mentions this in His Olivet Discourse in Matthew 24:15. He said that it would be a sign that would occur at the End of the Age — which was a reference to Daniel 9:27. However, it should be noted that while the seven-year period of Daniel (Da. 9:24-27) is frequently referred to as The Tribulation Period, it is difficult to find a single Scripture to support this designation of the term *Tribulation* Period, and this term should not be used as a synonym for Daniel's 70th Week. In other words, the word *Tribulation* and the term *The Great Tribulation* are not synonymous terms. The Great Tribulation refers only to the last half of The 70th Week of Daniel — not to the first half. As we study the Pre-Wrath position further, I want to approach this particular view in a simple and concise chronological method using Scripture parallels to determine the closest approximate timing of the Second Coming of Jesus Christ, the Resurrection, and the Rapture of the elect. Also, the study of Scripture parallels will help us to identify the correct timing and chronological order of the Beginning of Sorrows, which will, in turn, lead us to the Abomination of Desolation — mentioned in Daniel's 70th Week and the Olivet Discourse — which will lead us to The Great Tribulation, which will, in turn, lead us to the timing of the Cosmic Disturbance, which will, in turn, lead us to The Day of the Lord (i.e. The Wrath of God). I believe that the more accurate we are in identifying Scripture parallels, the more accurate we will be at identifying the chronology of The 70th Week of Daniel, the Olivet Discourse Prophecies, The Book of Revelation, 1 and 2 Thessalonians, The Book of Joel, and many other Books as well, and the more accurate we will be in determining the correct timing of the Rapture, the Resurrection, and Christ's Second Coming. I want everyone to understand that God has the final say with His Story about the End of the Age. It's His story, not ours. By using correct terminology, we will be able to better determine which End of the Age scenario is the closest to what God has actually taught us in His Precious Word. We want to focus only on the details revealed to us in the parallels passages found in God's Word to better identify and understand the best sequencing and chronology of Daniel's 70th Week as we add the additional details found in Christ's teachings in His Olivet Discourse Prophecies, and the Apostle John's vision of the Scroll and the seven Seals found in The Book of Revelation, and many more passages, as they are actually revealed to us by God the Holy Spirit Himself through His many parallel passages. The only way we can understand the specific details successfully to arrive at a correct understanding is by looking at all of the specific parallels found within the Holy Bible, as they pertain to each of the events in question, paying close attention to their correct context. By doing so we can create a basic foundation for the Rapture timeline to help us to better understand these critically important end-time prophesies more accurately. As we study this majorly important prophetic topic, I will be putting all the parallel passages in question together and arranging them in their chronological order using specific Scripture parallels. I will be organizing and comparing these teachings from the various above-mentioned Books of the Bible. Doing this will help us identify and understand the specific Biblical parallels in question. Understanding the 70th Week of Daniel and Scripture parallels is the key to unlocking specific details of the chronological timelines and sequences as they are revealed to us in the Bible, with regard to the End-of-the-Age Prophecies as God has revealed them to us. For the first time in my sixty-two years of living — I actually have a major advantage with interpreting and identifying Daniel's 70th-Week start date, at this particular moment in history. My advantage is in the fact that I now know when the 70th Week of Daniel began, due to both the Biblical and historical details, and the Work of the Holy Spirit, relative to details obtained through the Agenda 30's Sustainable Development Goals 7 (SDG7) Summit.[2] Because of the obvious identification of these parallels between Daniel's 70th Week and Agenda 30's SDG7, the start date has been revealed, which was September 18-19, 2023

---

2   https://sdg.iisd.org/events/sdg-summit-2023

(or its effective date), when the signing of the covenant between the anti-Christ, Israel, and the many (Da. 9:24-27), through the U. N. Agenda 30's aggressive SDG7 took place. I now understand that the many that is referred to in the Book of Daniel involves the 193 U.N. member states and the BRICS Financial-Treaty countries and their SDG7 17 Sustainable Development Goals agreement, which includes the Nation of Israel. Also, there is a linguistic parallel that occurred in Daniel's 70th-Week prophecy that further confirms my hypothesis and that is a linguistic parallel found within the Hebrew language that The Holy Spirit, through Daniel, chose to use, which is the word *"confirm"* in his text. The word in Hebrew that was used, according to many Hebrew scholars, is interpreted a "firm" and "mighty" agreement that also denotes a "re-commitment" or a "re-affirming" of a previously existing agreement, which is exactly what the Sustainable Development Goals/Agenda 30 is. It is actually a re-commitment of the 1992 Agenda 21 agreement. The fact that the Daniel 70th-Week prophecy tells us that the anti-Christ would both "confirm" and "re-affirm" a previous agreement is exactly correct, relative to the Biblical and historical context. According to the U.N. website, their leaders actually use the word *"aggressive"* when referring to the Agenda 30/SDG7 agreement (i.e. mighty and firm). It is a seven-year aggressive agreement between the United Nations (i.e. the anti-Christ), 193 United Nation member states (i.e. the many), and the Nation of Israel. See comparison chart below:

THE HISTORICAL & BIBLICAL COMPARISON	
The U.N. Agenda 30-SDG7	**Daniel 9:24–27**
Word: *"Aggressive"* used in marketing.	Word: English Hebrew *"Confirm"* = firm & mighty
Term: 7-year aggressive agreement	Term: 7-year firm & mighty agreement
Agenda 30-SDG7 aggressive agreement is a "re-commitment" or "re-affirming" of the Agenda 21 of 1992.	Hebrew word denotes a "re-commitment" or a "re-affirming" of a previously existing agreement.
Signed: the United Nations, Israel, and 193 nations	Signed: the anti-Christ, Israel, and the many

Chapter 2

Foundations for Understanding: The 70th Week

THE PURPOSE OF THE 70th WEEK OF DANIEL

Jesus promised that believers would experience tribulation in the world (John 16:33), but He and Daniel also predicted a unique time of the most severe and intense tribulation in human history that Jesus called *The Great Tribulation* and Daniel called it *a time of distress.*

Daniel 12:1

"Now at that time Michael, the great prince who stands guard over the sons of your people, will arise. And there will be a time of distress such as never occurred since there was a nation until that time; and at that time your people, everyone who is found written in the book, will be rescued."

Matthew 24:21

"For then there will be great tribulation, such as has not been from the beginning of the world until now, no, and never will be."

Daniel's 70th Week began when the unrevealed anti-Christ signed a covenant with Israel and the many (Dan 9:24-27). Not until the midpoint of Daniel's 70th Week when Michael is removed will the anti-Christ identity be revealed. During The 70th-Week-of-Daniel Judgments, close to 80% of the world's population will be destroyed, by the time the Beginning of Sorrows and The Great Tribulation are completed. If God had not cut the Great Tribulation short for the elect's sake, through a Cosmic Disturbance, no human beings would make it through alive (Mt. 24:22).

The two main reasons for The 70th Week of Daniel are these:

1. To prepare Israel for its Messiah.
2. To save and restore the Nation of Israel and to purify and rescue the Body of Christ.

Because the Jewish people were not ready to receive Christ the first time, God will prepare their hearts to receive Him the second time. God's Beginning of Sorrows and Great Tribulation will be poured out during Daniel's 70th Week and will make Israel ready to receive their Messiah and will purify and rescue the Body of Christ.

These are the reasons for the extreme suffering of Daniel's 70th Week: it will serve as God's discipline upon His chosen people, both Jews and Christians for their sin and rebellion. The 70th Week of Daniel is God's way to break the stubborn will of His chosen people of Israel, and also, in the Body of Christ, to separate the sheep from the goats and the wheat from the chaff, and to prepare His Chosen people to receive their Messiah. Through the horrible suffering of The Great Tribulation, God will remove the spiritual blinders from the Nation of Israel and the Body of Christ. When that happens, Israel will become a believing nation and God will have fulfilled His promises to Israel (Jer. 31:31-34), and the Body of Christ will be purified (Da. 12:10, Ps. 66:10, 1Jn.1:9).

Once you understand Daniel's 70th Week, you will begin to see more clearly how specific sequenced events found in Jesus' Olivet Discourse Prophecies, the Apostle John's Book of Revelation Chapters 6-8, the Apostle Paul's 1 and 2 Thessalonians, and other books, fit together perfectly with Daniel's 70th-Week timeline, relative to the End-of-the-Age Prophecies, which include the Rapture, Resurrection, and Christ's Second Coming (Mt. 24:10-11, 30, 31, 37, 39; 2Th. 2: 1-4).

Although Daniel's 70th Week precisely gives us the time when the prophecy would begin to be fulfilled, which was at the signing of the recent seven-year covenant between the anti-Christ, the Nation of Israel, and the many, I will not be getting involved with the accurate and amazing mathematical calculations of Daniel's prophecy in this book. But if you want to study Daniel's 70th-Week prophecy, please go to Josh McDowell's book entitled

The New Evidence That Demands a Verdict, pages 197–201, for a detailed explanation. The reason that I will not be spending any time on Daniel's precise mathematical calculations of his 70th Week is that, in my opinion, it is not necessary at this time because for the first time in Earth's history we have identified the seven-year covenant start date between the anti-Christ, the Nation of Israel, and the many. The United Nations' Agenda 30 agreement was signed at the SDG7 Summit on September 18-19, 2023 (or its effective date). What this means is that, if this hypothesis is correct, then The 70th Week of Daniel has begun! The 70th Week Prophecy of Daniel makes references to the Messiah and specifies the timing and details of Jesus' ministry. It is one of the most amazing Messianic Prophecies in the entire Bible (Da. 9:24-27). Jesus was talking to His disciples about Daniel's 70th-Week prophesies to show them that Daniel's 70th-Week prophecies were being and would be fulfilled through Him and that the destruction of Jerusalem and the Temple would follow the First Coming of Israel's Messiah — Himself — which means that, according to Daniel's prophecy, the Messiah will be "cut-off" (killed) before the destruction of the Second Temple. Therefore, the Messiah had to appear and die before the destruction of Jerusalem and the Temple, which eventually occurred in A.D. 70. Christ specifically told His disciples to *understand* the prophecies of Daniel — and we must understand them as well. The Book of Daniel is an amazing timeline by which we can parallel all the other prophecies found in the Bible, and doing so adds many more details, such as the passage-parallel information found in Jesus' Olivet Discourse in Matthew 24 and the Apostle John's Book of Revelation 6-8 and his vision about the Scroll and the seven Seals. There are many more prophetic sequences found in Scripture that parallel with Daniel's 70th Week, some of which we will be discussing in this book. We will look at the Scripture parallels in order to complement and further clarify these events in more detail. Through this process we will get a greater understanding through the details discovered by the parallel passages that will help us to sequence the logical progression within this critically important seven-year period. Let's explore the events of the above-mentioned Books of the Bible, so that we can determine the chronological sequence of the events described in The 70th Week of

Daniel. One of the most important prophetic passages in the whole Bible was given to the prophet Daniel by the angel Gabriel and revealed to us in Daniel 9:24-27. This amazing prophecy is essential for the correct understanding of the chronological sequencing of this End-Times scenario. The correct understanding of The 70th Week of Daniel will lead to the approximate timing of the Rapture of the Church, the Second Coming of Jesus Christ, the Day of the Lord, and other important events. For our Bible study, I will be using the following Scriptures to construct a proper exegesis for my hermeneutic: Daniel 9:24-27; Matthew 24:15-31; Joel 2:29-30; 1 Thessalonians 4:15, 17; 2 Thessalonians 2:1-9; 2:5; Revelation 6- 8.

Daniel 9:24-27

> *"24Seventy weeks are decreed for your people and your holy city to stop their transgression, to put an end to sin, to make atonement for iniquity, to bring in everlasting righteousness, to seal up vision and prophecy, and to anoint the Most Holy Place. 25Know and understand this: From the issuing of the decree to restore and rebuild Jerusalem, until the Messiah, the Prince, there will be seven weeks and sixty-two weeks. It will be rebuilt with streets and a trench, but in times of distress. 26Then after the sixty-two weeks, the Messiah will be cut off and will have nothing, and the people of the prince who is to come will destroy the city and the sanctuary. The end will come like a flood, and until the end there will be war; desolations have been decreed. 27And he will confirm a covenant with many for one week, but in the middle of the week he will put an end to sacrifice and offering. And on the wing of the temple will come the abomination that causes desolation, until the decreed destruction is poured out upon him."*

The 70th Week of Daniel is a Messianic Prophecy that announces the consequences of Israel's rejection of their Messiah. The prophet Daniel wrote his 70th-Week Prophecy about 2,600 years ago, and it is the very backbone to Biblical eschatology. Most eschatological scholars say that the Book of Daniel is mandatory study and is the key to understanding all the End-Time Bible Prophecy. Once you begin to understand Daniel's 70th Week, then you will begin to see more clearly how specific events such as Jesus' Olivet Discourse Prophecies in Matthew 24, the Apostle John's Book of Revelation 6-8, the Apostle Paul's 1 and 2 Thessalonians and 1 Corinthians 15, as well as other books, all fit perfectly together. I will show you this as we overlay the above-mentioned passages with Daniel's 70th Week, as we learn the precise chronological sequencing for the Rapture, the Resurrection, and Christ's Second Coming. For example, after Jesus told His disciples about the signs that will occur prior to His Second Coming and the End of the Age, and that the Words He spoke are True, He told them that, when these signs appear in heaven, His return would be near. Also, He said that all this would happen within a last specific generation, which this hypothesis declares is the 2023-2030 generation, (Mt. 24:33-35; Mk. 13:28-31; Lk. 21:29-33). What are the actual signs that will appear in heaven prior to Christ's Second Coming? Christ tells us in Matthew 24:29.

Matthew 24:29

"²⁹Immediately after the tribulation of those days: 'The sun will be darkened, and the moon will not give its light; the stars will fall from the sky, and the powers of the heavens will be shaken.'"

So through passage-paralleling, we have learned that after The Great Tribulation, The Cosmic Disturbance and the appearance of the Son of Man in heaven will make the whole non-believing world mourn. God's Word is so consistent, and the reason God's Word is so consistent is that it is True. Jesus told His disciples that The Cosmic Disturbance would be a sign in the heavens that would occur just prior to His Second Coming.

Matthew 24:30-31

"³⁰At that time the sign of the Son of Man will appear in heaven, and all the tribes of the earth will mourn. They will see the Son of Man coming on the clouds of heaven, with power and great glory. ³¹And He will send out His angels with a loud trumpet call, and they will gather His elect from the four winds, from one end of the heavens to the other."

According to Scripture, Christ's Second Coming will occur after The Cosmic Disturbance. The passage-parallel method of study creates additional information discoveries which are beneficial in our understanding. Jesus also told His disciples that when you see all these things that His return is near. He also told His disciples that when these signs occur that they would occur within a specific generation, which (I tell you again) this hypothesis declares is the 2023-2030 generation.

Matthew 24:33-35

"33So also, when you see all these things, you will know that He is near, right at the door. 34Truly I tell you, this generation will not pass away until all these things have happened. 35Heaven and earth will pass away, but My words will never pass away."

When we passage-parallel these above Scriptures with Daniel's 70th Week and John's vision in the Book of Revelation, Chapter 6, we can create a greater picture of the events in question as we pinpoint the precise moment of the Cosmic Disturbance relative to Daniel's 70th Week. According to Revelation 6:12-13, the Cosmic Disturbance will occur at the sixth Seal. Also, there will be a great earthquake and the stars will fall to the earth.

Revelation 6:12-13

"And when I saw the Lamb open the sixth seal, there was a great earthquake, and the sun became black like sackcloth of goat hair, and the whole moon turned blood red, 13and the stars of the sky fell to the earth like unripe figs dropping from a tree shaken by a great wind."

Chapter 3

The Seven Seals, Seven Trumpets, and Seven Bowls — in Sequence

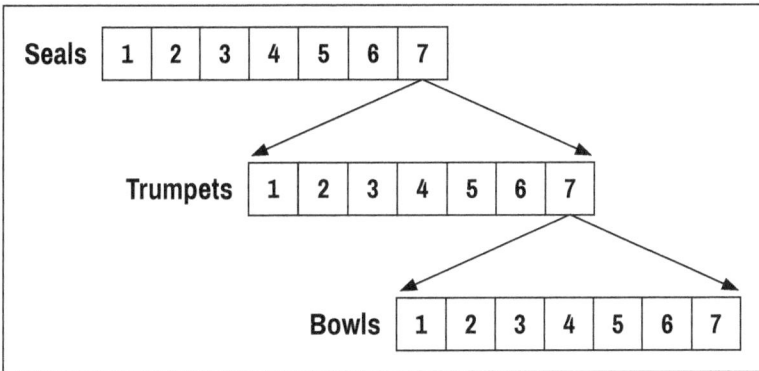

The Seven Trumpets and Seven Bowls will happen in sequence, or consecutively, not concurrently, after the seven Seals are removed from the Scroll itself (Rev. 8:10-11:19; 16:21; 18:1-24). They do not all occur at the same time. They occur one after another. The key thing to remember is that the Scroll itself cannot be open until all the seven Seals are broken. The Seals are on the outside of the Scroll, and the seven Trumpets and seven Bowls are God's judgments contained on the inside of the Scroll.

Seven Seals

First Seal	Second Seal	Third Seal
The White Horse: Anti-Christ, False Christ, comes with a bow (with no arrows) and a crown is given to him. He goes forth conquering and to conquer (Rev. 6:1-2), through diplomacy, not with a sword, in the beginning.	**The Red Horse:** War takes peace from the earth with a great sword (Rev. 6:3-4). It is not clear what kind(s) of war(s) are referred to at this time, but they could possibly represent either international war(s) or civil strife.	**The Black Horse:** Famine comes holding scales. A voice says a day's food will cost a day's wages, and don't hurt the oil and wine (Rev. 6:5-6). This famine could be caused as a result of war, severe inflation, food production shortages, or a combination of all three.
Fourth Seal	**Fifth Seal**	**Sixth Seal**
The Pale Horse: Death comes to ¼ of the earth. Hell follows this horse. They kill with the sword, hunger, plague, and beasts (Rev. 6:7-8). Possibly these ¼ of the earth's population deaths are accumulated from the first four Seals.	**Martyrdom:** Souls of those slain are seen under the altar. They are given white robes (Rev. 6:9-11). These are the Jews and Christians killed and/or martyred during Daniel's 70th Week. The Two Witnesses begin their ministry (Rev. 11:3).	**Cosmic Disturbance:** Great earthquake, sun is blackened, moon turns blood red, stars fall from sky, moving of mountains and islands (Rev. 6:12-17; Mt. 24:29), the Second Coming, Rapture, and Resurrection occur (Mt. 24:30-31; 1Th. 4:16-18; Rev. 1:7).
Christ's Second Coming, Rapture, and Resurrection	**Seventh Seal** Silence in Heaven happens for half an hour (Rev. 8:12). The Day of the Lord and God's Wrath begin (Rev. 8:1-8).	

The Timing of the Seven Trumpets and Seven Bowls

The Seven Trumpets and Seven Bowls will begin after the Seventh Seal is removed from the Scroll and its contents are revealed. The contents of the Scroll are the Seven Trumpets and Bowls of God's Judgments.

The Seven Trumpets and Seven Bowls revealed to us through the Scripture's below are not understood in their complete details at this time, only partially. What we know is these Judgments from God will be horrific and catastrophic after the sixth Seal. Therefore, the martyred and those who experienced the rapture (ICo. 15: 50-57) will not be subject to the wrath of God, but instead will be attending the Marriage Supper of the Lamb in Heaven (Rev. 19:7-9; 1Co. 3:10-15).

Seven Trumpets

First Trumpet	Second Trumpet	Third Trumpet
Hail and fire are mingled with blood, 1/3 of the earth and all green grass are burned up (Rev. 8:6-7).	Something like a great mountain burning with fire is cast into the sea, 1/3 of the sea becomes blood, 1/3 of the living creatures of the sea die, and 1/3 of the ships are destroyed (Rev. 8:8-9).	Wormwood, a great star from heaven, burning like a torch, falls upon 1/3 of the rivers and springs of water. A third of the waters are made bitter, and 1/3 of the men die from the waters (Rev. 8:10- 11).
Fourth Trumpet	**Fifth Trumpet**	**Sixth Trumpet**
A third of the sun, moon, and stars are struck and darkened so 1/3 of the day and night do not shine (Rev. 8:12-13).	First Woe! Locusts like horses prepared for battle appear. A star from heaven is given the key to the bottomless pit and it is opened. Locusts come up and sting for five months the men that do not have the seal of the living God on their foreheads (Rev. 9:1-12).	Second Woe! Four angels bound at the Euphrates River are released to kill 1/3 of mankind (Rev. 9:13-21).
	Seventh Trumpet	
	Third Woe! The kingdom of this world and the Kingdom of our Lord are become one. The 24 elders worship. The temple of God in heaven is opened, and there are flashes of lightning, peals of thunder, and a great hailstorm (Rev. 11:15-19).	

Seven Bowls

First Bowl	Second Bowl	Third Bowl
Horrible sores are on the ones that have the mark of the beast and worship his image (Rev. 16:2).	Sea becomes blood like that of a dead man, and every living thing in the sea dies (Rev. 16:3).	The rivers and the springs of waters become blood (Rev. 16:4).
Fourth Bowl	**Fifth Bowl**	**Sixth Bowl**
The sun is given the power to scorch men with fire (Rev. 16:8-9).	The beast's kingdom becomes darkened, and the people gnaw their tongues because of their pain (Rev. 16:10-11).	The Euphrates River dries up so that the way is prepared for the kings of the East. Unclean spirits like frogs come out of the dragon, beast, and false prophet to perform signs to gather the kings of the world for the war of the great Day of God Almighty (Rev. 16:12-14).
	Seventh Bowl	
	The Voice out of the temple says, "It is done!" Lightning, thunder, and a great earthquake occur. The city is split into three parts. The islands flee, the mountains cannot be found, and hailstones almost 100 pounds in weight come down on men who blaspheme God (Rev. 16:17-21).	

1. The White Horse — who wears a crown and has a bow with no arrows — and the first Seal are synonymous with the man of sin/anti-Christ who goes fourth conquering through diplomacy in the beginning (Rev. 6:1-2; Mt. 24:4-5; Mk. 13:5-6; Lk. 21:8).

2. The Red Horse and the second Seal are synonymous with wars and peace taken from the Earth and could possibly mean international wars and/or civil strife (Rev. 6:3-4; Mt. 24:6-7; Mk, 13:7-8; Lk. 21:9-10).

3. The Black Horse and the third Seal are synonymous with famines — including a measure of wheat for a penny — possibly caused by wars, food production shortages, and inflation, or a combination of all the above-mentioned causes — pestilence, and earthquakes (Rev. 6:5-6; Mt. 24:7; Mk. 13:8; Lk. 21:11).

4. The Pale Horse and the fourth Seal are synonymous with death in ¼ of the earth's population possibly caused by all the deaths accumulated from all four Seals combined (Rev. 6:7-8).

5. The fifth Seal is in regard to martyrs, false prophets, deception, and the beginning of the Great Tribulation. The Two Witnesses begin their ministry (Rev. 11:3), and the Gospel is preached (Da. 12:1; Rev. 6:9-11; 12:17; Mt. 24:9-14; 21-22; Mk. 13:9-13; Lk. 21:11-19).

6. The sixth Seal is in regard to the Cosmic Disturbance — darkening of the sun and moon; falling of stars; Elijah's returning before the Day of the Lord (Mal. 4:5); sealing of the 144,000; and Second Coming of Christ, Rapture, and Resurrection (Rev. 1:7; 6:12-17; 14:1-15:4; 22:12; Mt. 24:14, 29-31; Mk. 13:13, 24-27; Lk. 21:25-28; 1Th. 4:16-17).

7. The seventh Seal is the Day of the Lord, or the Wrath of God for the lost (Is.13:9) and the Day of Christ for the saved (Ph. 1:6). Prior to the Day of the Lord, Heaven will have one-half hour of silence (Rev. 8:1), just before God's Judgments on Earth begin (Rev. 8:1-6; Rev. 15:6-16:1).

8. The seven Trumpets and Bowls will happen in sequence, or consecutively, not concurrently, after the seven Seals (Rev. 8:10-11:19; 16:21; 18:1-24). They do not all occur at the same time. They occur one after another.
9. Babylon will fall in one hour (Rev. 18:1-24).
10. At the Battle of Armageddon Christ comes on a White Horse with many royal crowns and a sword to judge the nations (Rev. 19:11-21).
11. Kingdoms in the New Earth will be given to the Saints (Rev. 21:1-6).

Chapter 4

The Covenant, Abomination, and the Man of Lawlessness

The Abomination of Desolation is a phrase that is used several times throughout Scripture. It is a reference to the desecration of the sacred Temple in Jerusalem. This event has happened many times throughout history and will occur one more time in the near future (Da. 9:27; 11:31; 12:11; Mt. 24:15-16; Mk. 13:14; Lk. 21:20).

The 70th Week of Daniel has begun with the signing of a seven-year covenant between Israel, the unrevealed anti-Christ, and the many — but after 3½ years into the agreement and Michael is removed, the anti-Christ will put a stop to all sacrifices and offerings and will erect an image of himself in the Temple and demand that the Jews, Christians, and all of the other people in the world worship him as God. This is known as the Abomination of Desolation. We read about this in Daniel 9:27.

Daniel 9:27

> *"27And he will confirm a covenant with many for one week, but in the middle of the week he will put an end to sacrifice and offering. And on the wing of the temple will come the abomination that causes desolation, until the decreed destruction is poured out upon him."*

The seven-year covenant will be halted by the anti-Christ at the halfway point — 3½ years into the 70th Week of Daniel. The Abomination of Desolation will occur, and the anti-Christ is revealed. We read about this event in Matthew 24:15. Jesus actually refers to the Abomination of Desolation mentioned by the prophet Daniel.

Matthew 24:15

> "15 So when you see standing in the holy place 'the abomination of desolation,' described by the prophet Daniel (let the reader understand),"

The Man of Lawlessness Revealed

The man of lawlessness is revealed when he sits in God's Temple declaring himself to be God and sets up the abomination that causes desolation, which occurs at the 3½-year mark of Daniel's 70th Week (Da. 9:27; 11:31; Mt. 24:15; Mk. 13:14; 2Th. 2:3-4). Up to this midpoint in the 70th Week of Daniel, the anti-Christ's identity is not revealed to the world. The reason for this is that he is and will have been working essentially behind the scenes at the top level at the United Nation SDG7 Organization for 3½ years until the Abomination of Desolation occurs. It is at the Abomination of Desolation that the actual identity of the person of the anti-Christ will be revealed. I think we may or may not be surprised. In other words, he could be someone we have seen before and suspected, or he could be someone who we had not known or suspected. We will have to wait until 3½ years into Daniel's 70th Week to find out for sure who the anti-Christ actually is.

Chapter 5

The Scroll and the Seven Seals

We must keep in mind that the Seals Jesus breaks are not the Wrath of God. The Wrath of God is the contents, or the message, inside the Scroll. After Jesus has broken all seven Seals, then the content of the Scroll can be revealed. Inside the Scroll are the seven Trumpets and the seven Bowls of God's Judgments. They are the Wrath of God (i.e. The Day of the Lord). The Scroll and the seven Seals, the Olivet Discourse, and the 70th Week of Daniel are the keys to unlocking the chronological sequence and the timing of the End-of-the-Age Prophecies, the Rapture, and the Second Coming of Jesus Christ. In order for us to understand the context and see the logical progression of these future seven-year events more clearly, we will need to explore the chronological order and parallels found within Scripture to better understand the sequence of these major Biblical events. We must take a look at the chronological sequence of these events which will lead us to the correct timing of the Rapture, Christ's Second Coming, the Cosmic Disturbance, and the Great Tribulation and God's Wrath. We also need to look at the Book of Revelation Chapters 5 and 6 to gather some clues to help us better understand the chronological sequencing of the Scroll and the seven Seals. We read in The Book of Revelation Chapter 5, that the Apostle John had a vision and he saw a scroll that had seven seals wrapped around it in the hand of God as He was seated on His Throne in Heaven. At first John was amazed by the fact that there was a universal search made to find someone worthy to open the Scroll but that no one could be found. The Apostle John wept loudly because he knew that if there was no one found worthy to open the Scroll, then all hope would be lost. "Then one of the elders said to me [John], 'Do not weep! Behold, the Lion of the tribe of Judah, the Root of David, has triumphed to open the scroll and its 7 seals.' Then I saw a Lamb who appeared to have been slain, standing in the center of the throne...." (Rev. 5:5-6). The Person that was found worthy was Jesus Christ. Now keep in mind that this Scroll was no ordinary Scroll; in a legal sense, this Scroll was the title deed to Earth. Jesus Christ was the God-Man Who was worthy to open the Scroll. The reason Jesus Christ was worthy was because He redeemed people to God through His shed blood on His cross. This All-Sufficient Sacrifice — His Son, Jesus — was God the Father's price for mankind's redemption. That's why Christ is depicted in the Apostle John's vision as the Lamb Who was slain. I will show you that — when it is all said and done — according to The Holy Bible, Jesus Christ will come back for His elect when the sixth Seal is opened (Mt. 24:29-30; Rev.6:12-17) before The Day of the Lord (i.e. The 7th Seal). I find that people are very surprised when they find out that the references to Christ's Second Coming outnumber the references found in the Holy Bible about Christ's First Coming by a ratio of eight to one. Scholars have identified 1,845 different Biblical references about the Second Coming of Jesus Christ. In the Old Testament seventeen Books mention Christ's Second Coming. In the New Testament we find 23 of the 27 Books refer to Christ's Second Coming. In the New Testament we find seven out of 10 chapters refer to Christ's Second Coming: that's one out of every 30 verses that refer to His Second Coming.

Chapter 6

Seals 1-6, The Olivet Discourse and The Book of Revelation Parallels

In Matthew 24:3, Jesus Christ was with His disciples on the Mount of Olives when they asked Him what would be the sign of His Second Coming and the End of the age. His answer to His disciples is recorded in the Holy Bible and is referred to as The Olivet Discourse Prophecies. The Olivet Discourse Prophecies are an orderly and detailed prophetic teaching by Jesus Christ, and the subject of this teaching is about the End of the Age, and is addressed to Israel and the Church, and parallel passages are found in these Books as well: Mark 13:1-37; Luke 21:5-36; and Matthew 24:1-25, 46.

Matthew 24:3

> "³*While Jesus was sitting on the Mount of Olives, the disciples came to Him privately. 'Tell us,' they said, 'when will all this happen, and what will be the sign of Your coming and of the end of the age?'*"

Now I want to layout the events of The Great Tribulation in a concise, single-column format according to Matthew and the Book of Revelation. The time of the Great Tribulation will include the following:

- Persecution and martyrdom of Christians and Jews (Mt. 24:9; Rev. 6:9; 13:7).
- Apostasy — the turning away of many Christians and Jews from their faith (Mt. 24:10, 12; Rev. 2:3).

- Many false prophets (Mt. 24:11, 24; Rev. 19:20).
- Many people's deception (Mt. 24:11, 24; Rev, 13:13-14; 19:20).
- Increase of wickedness (Mt. 24:12; Rev. 13:8).
- The preaching of the Gospel to every nation (Mt. 24:14; Rev. 14:6).

The Prepared and the Unprepared Comparison

When we compare the prepared with the unprepared in Scripture, we see a dramatic difference between the response of those who are prepared and those who are not. Those of us who are prepared will stand up confident, unafraid, and expectant, knowing that our redemption is drawing near (Lk. 21:28).

The unprepared will be perplexed and in anguish, terrified, and apprehensive. They will know that fearful and horrible events are taking place on the earth (Lk. 21:25-26).

THE PARALLELS THAT ARE BEING FOLLOWED BETWEEN MATTHEW 24 AND REVELATION 6 ARE EXACTLY THE SAME CONTEXT IN EACH PASSAGE. WHEN WE CONNECT THE PARALLEL PASSAGES, THE ADDITIONAL INFORMATION IS THEN REVEALED.

FALSE CHRISTS

Matthew 24:5

"⁵For many will come in My name, claiming, 'I am the Christ,' and will deceive many."

Revelation 6:1-2

"¹Then I watched as the Lamb opened one of the seven seals, and I heard one of the four living creatures say in a thunderous voice, 'Come!' ²So I looked and saw a white horse, and its rider had a bow. And he was given a crown, and rode out to conquer and defeat."

WAR

Matthew 24:6-7

"⁶You will hear of wars and rumors of wars, but see to it that you are not alarmed. These things must happen, but the end is still to come.

⁷Nation will rise against nation, and kingdom against kingdom."

Revelation 6:3-4

"³And when the Lamb opened the second seal, I heard the second living creature say, 'Come!' ⁴Then another horse went forth. It was bright red, and its rider was granted permission to take peace from the earth and to make men slay one another. And he was given a great sword."

FAMINE

Matthew 24:7b

"⁷ᵇThere will be famines and earthquakes in various places."

Revelation 6:5-6

"⁵And when the Lamb opened the third seal, I heard the third living creature say, 'Come!' Then I looked and saw a black horse, and its rider held in his hand a pair of scales. ⁶And I heard what sounded like a voice from among the four living creatures, saying, 'A quart of wheat for a denarius, and three quarts of barley for a denarius, and do not waste the oil and the wine.'"

PESTILENCE

Matthew 24:7c-8

"⁷ᶜ pestilences, and earthquakes, in divers places. ⁸All these are the beginning of birth pains."

Revelation 6:7-8

"⁷And when the Lamb opened the fourth seal, I heard the voice of the fourth living creature say, 'Come!' ⁸Then I looked and saw a pale horse. Its rider's name was Death, and Hades followed close behind. And they were given authority over a fourth of the earth, to kill by sword, by famine, by plague, and by the beasts of the earth."

MARTYRDOM

Matthew 24:9-11

"⁹Then they will deliver you over to be persecuted and killed, and you will be hated by all nations because of My name. ¹⁰At that time many will fall away and will betray and hate one another, ¹¹and many false prophets will arise and mislead many."

Revelation 6:9-11

"⁹And when the Lamb opened the fifth seal, I saw under the altar the souls of those who had been slain for the word of God and for the testimony they had upheld. ¹⁰And they cried out in a loud voice, 'How long, O Lord, holy and true, until You avenge our blood and judge those who dwell upon the earth?' ¹¹Then each of them was given a white robe and told to rest a little while longer, until the full number of their fellow servants, their brothers, were killed, just as they had been killed."

COSMIC DISTURBANCE

Matthew 24:29

"²⁹Immediately after the tribulation of those days: 'The sun will be darkened, and the moon will not give its light; the stars will fall from the sky, and the powers of the heavens will be shaken.'"

Revelation 6:12-13

"12And when I saw the Lamb open the 6th seal, there was a great earthquake, and the sun became black like sackcloth of goat hair, and the whole moon turned blood red, 13and the stars of the sky fell to the earth, like unripe figs dropping from a tree shaken by a great wind."

Here is the proof-text parallel chart between Matthew 24 and Revelation 6. When we lay Jesus' Olivet Discourse from Matthew 24 over the Apostle John's Book of Revelation chapter 6, they align perfectly.

MATTHEW 24		REVELATION 6
Mt. 24:5	FALSE CHRIST/ANTI-CHRIST	Rev. 6:1-2
Mt. 24:6-7	WAR	Rev. 6:3-4
Mt. 24:7b	FAMINE	Rev. 6: 5-6
Mt. 24:7c-8	PESTILENCE	Rev. 6:7-8
Mt. 24:9	MARTYRDOM	Rev. 6:9-11
Mt. 24:29	COSMIC DISTURBANCE	Rev. 6:12-13

Chapter 7

The Jesus-and-Paul Passage-Parallels

When we compare the passage parallels of Jesus' and the Apostle Paul's teachings on Jesus' Second Coming we find additional information which creates a fuller and more detailed picture of the events in question.

About Jesus' Second Coming

Matthew 24:30

> *"30At that time the sign of the Son of Man will appear in heaven, and all the tribes of the earth will mourn. They will see the Son of Man coming on the clouds of heaven, with power and great glory."*

1 Thessalonians 4:16

> *"16For the Lord Himself will descend from heaven with a loud command, with the voice of an archangel, and with the trumpet of God, and the dead in Christ will be the first to rise."*

Jesus Located in the Clouds

Matthew 24:30

> *"30At that time the sign of the Son of Man will appear in heaven, and all the tribes of the earth will mourn. They will see the Son of Man coming on the clouds of heaven, with power and great glory."*

1 Thessalonians 4:17

"17After that, we who are alive and remain will be caught up together with them in the clouds to meet the Lord in the air. And so we will always be with the Lord."

A Trumpet Sounds Before the Rapture

Matthew 24:31

"31And He will send out His angels with a loud trumpet call, and they will gather His elect from the four winds, from one end of the heavens to the other."

1 Thessalonians 4:16

"16For the Lord Himself will descend from heaven with a loud command, with the voice of an archangel, and with the trumpet of God, and the dead in Christ will be the first to rise."

Christians Are Raptured

Matthew 24:31, 40-41

"31And He will send out His angels with a loud trumpet call, and they will gather His elect from the four winds, from one end of the heavens to the other. 40Two men will be in the field: one will be taken and the other left. 41Two women will be grinding at the mill: one will be taken and the other left."

1 Thessalonians 4:17

"17After that, we who are alive and remain will be caught up together with them in the clouds to meet the Lord in the air. And so we will always be with the Lord."

People of the World Caught Unaware of Jesus' Coming

Matthew 24:39

> "*39And they were oblivious, until the flood came and swept them all away. So will it be at the coming of the Son of Man.*"

1 Thessalonians 5:3

> "*3While people are saying, 'Peace and security,' destruction will come upon them suddenly, like labor pains on a pregnant woman, and they will not escape.*"

Jesus' Coming Brings Destruction and Judgment to the World

Matthew 24:39

> "*39And they were oblivious, until the flood came and swept them all away. So will it be at the coming of the Son of Man.*"

1 Thessalonians 5:3

> "*3While people are saying, 'Peace and security,' destruction will come upon them suddenly, like labor pains on a pregnant woman, and they will not escape.*"

People of the World Are Living Life As Normal When Jesus Comes Back

Matthew 24:37-39

> "*37As it was in the days of Noah, so will it be at the coming of the Son of Man. 38For in the days before the flood, people were eating and drinking, marrying and giving in marriage, up to the day Noah entered the ark. 39And they were oblivious, until the flood came and swept them all away. So will it be at the coming of the Son of Man.*"

1 Thessalonians 5:3

> "*3While people are saying, 'Peace and security,' destruction will come upon them suddenly, like labor pains on a pregnant woman, and they will not escape.*"

Jesus' Coming Will Be Like a Thief in the Night to the Unprepared

Matthew 24:43, 48-50

> "*43But understand this: If the homeowner had known in which watch of the night the thief was coming, he would have kept watch and would not have let his house be broken into. 48But suppose that servant is wicked and says in his heart, 'My master will be away a long time.' 49And he begins to beat his fellow servants and to eat and drink with drunkards. 50The master of that servant will come on a day he does not expect and at an hour he does not anticipate.*"

1 Thessalonians 5:2, 4

> "*2For you are fully aware that the Day of the Lord will come like a thief in the night. 4But you, brothers, are not in the darkness so that this day should overtake you like a thief.*"

Believers Exhorted to Keep Watch and to Be Ready for Jesus' Coming

Matthew 24:42-44

> "*42Therefore keep watch, because you do not know the day on which your Lord will come. 43But understand this: If the homeowner had known in which watch of the night the thief was coming, he would have kept watch and would not have let his house be broken into. 44For this reason, you also must be ready, because the Son of Man will come at an hour you do not expect.*"

1 Thessalonians 5:4-6

"⁴But you, brothers, are not in the darkness so that this day should over-take you like a thief. ⁵For you are all sons of the light and sons of the day; we do not belong to the night or to the darkness. ⁶So then, let us not sleep as the others do, but let us remain awake and sober."

When we parallel Daniel's 70th Week with the Apostle John's Book of Revelation chapter 6, they align perfectly.

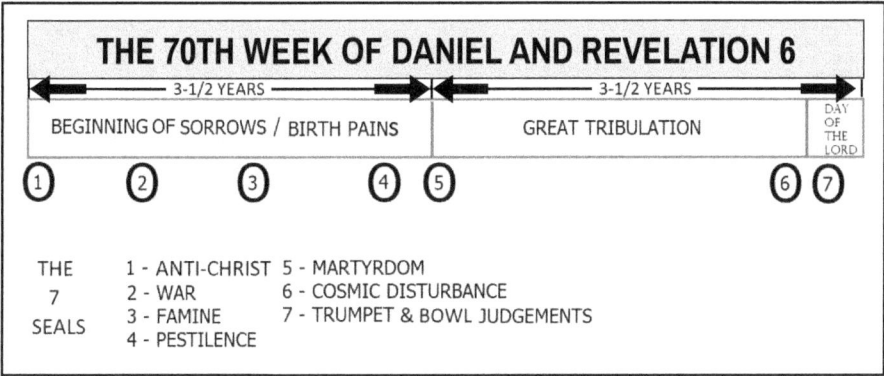

Also, when we parallel Jesus' Olivet Discourse Prophecies with the Book of Revelation, we see that they align perfectly as well.

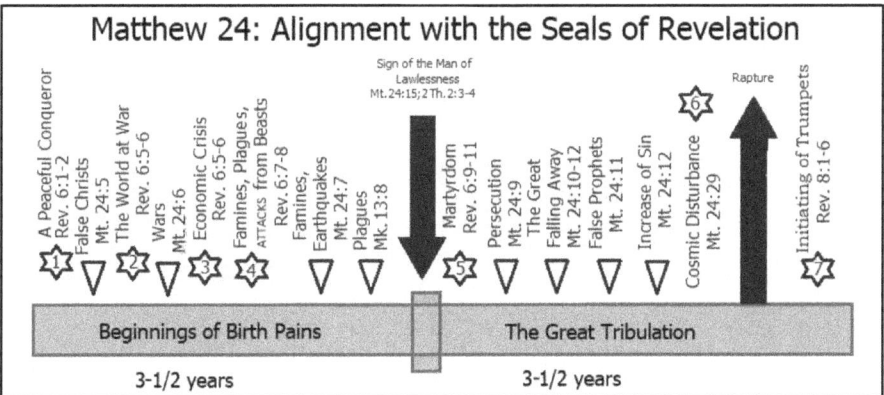

Chapter 8

The Cosmic Disturbance Parallels

THE PARALLELS BEING FOLLOWED BELOW ARE EXACTLY THE SAME CONTEXT IN EACH PASSAGE — IN THIS CASE, THE SUN BEING DARKENED, THE MOON TURNING BLOOD RED, AND THE DAY OF THE LORD. WHEN WE CONNECT THE PARALLEL PASSAGES, THE ADDITIONAL INFORMATION IS THEN REVEALED.

Parallel Passages

In the Bible, a parallel passage is comparing a passage of a story that is told in more than one place of the Bible, which describes the same event with different details. Comparing parallel passages in the Bible becomes a helpful tool in identifying additional information of a particular Biblical story with more details. The Bible frequently describes the same stories from different points of view. Parallel passages give a more complete picture of a specific event. Studying parallel passages is a method that can help the student of the Bible grasp God's Word with deeper understanding.

The passages found in The Book of Joel Chapter 2, The Book of Matthew Chapter 24, and The Book of Revelation Chapter 6 chronologically give us some very important clues as to the identity and timing of specific Biblical events. These passages confirm that The Cosmic Disturbance will occur at the sixth Seal and that it will come before The Day of the Lord (i.e. God's Wrath). The Book of Joel Chapter 2:31 parallels nicely with the Cosmic Disturbance event found in The Book of Matthew Chapter 24:29 and

Revelation 6:12-13. Also, The Book of Matthew 24:30 adds an additional piece of information — that The Son of Man will come "on the clouds of heaven, with power and great glory." The Book of Joel also reveals to us that The Cosmic Disturbance will happen before the Day of the Lord (i.e. the seventh Seal). These Bible passages parallel perfectly. What we have learned through our study of these above-mentioned verses is that The Cosmic Disturbance will occur at the sixth Seal, just before The Day of the Lord, and The Second Coming of Jesus Christ will also occur at the sixth Seal, prior to The Day of the Lord (i.e. God's Wrath). In summary, The Rapture, Resurrection, The Second Coming of Jesus Christ, and The Cosmic Disturbance all occur at the sixth Seal. We will dig a little deeper into the meaning of the term "The Day of the Lord" in the form of a chart in this book. When we do, we will learn through Revelation 8:1-6 that God's Judgments coming to the occupants of Earth at that time will be so bad there will be silence in heaven for about half an hour before God begins His Judgments through the seven Trumpets and seven Bowls.

Thinking about the fact that the Book of Daniel was written in the first half of the second century B.C., The Book of Matthew was written around A.D. 55–A.D. 65, The Book of Revelation was written around A.D. 66–A.D. 69, and The Book of Joel was written around 835 B.C., I'm amazed at how Scripture completely validates itself through its cohesiveness, coherency, and consistency. The Supernatural Intervention and Confirmation of the Holy Bible is easily recognized, but sometimes hard to understand. What these parallels tell us is that Christ's Second Coming will not be a Pre-Tribulation or a Mid-Tribulation event. Also, these passages show us, along with The 70th Week of Daniel, that Christ's Second Coming will occur sometime in the last part of the second half of Daniel's 70th Week. The teachings of Jesus in the Book of Matthew Chapter 24 and Apostle John in the Book of Revelation Chapter 6 also concur. For obvious reasons, these passages alone create a serious problem for the Pre-Tribulation adherents and their Eschatological positions. What I mean by this statement is the parallel passages found show us there are things that must take place prior to Christ's Rapture and Second Coming, which means the Bible does not support the Pre-Tribulation imminency doctrine because there are events that must occur prior to Christ's return. What the Bible actually teaches is expectancy of Christ's Rapture and Return. We need to be watching and be ready. I don't think it is helpful for us to try to ignore these above-mentioned Biblical teachings or attempt to try to explain them away.

Let's take a look again at the passage parallels found in the Bible about The Cosmic Disturbance, and you decide their plausibility.

Joel tells us here that The Cosmic Disturbance will occur <u>before</u> The Great Day of the Lord.

Joel 2:30-32

*"30I will show wonders in the heavens and on the earth, blood and fire and columns of smoke. 31The sun will be turned to darkness and the moon to blood **before** the coming of the great and awesome day of the LORD. 32And everyone who calls on the name of the LORD will be saved; for on Mount Zion and in Jerusalem there will be deliverance, as the LORD has promised, among the remnant called by the LORD."*

This next parallel is from Matthew 24:29-31. We identify The Cosmic Disturbance here as I have mentioned previously. In this passage from Jesus' Sermon on the Mount of Olives, He explains to His disciples about the signs of His Second Coming and End of the Age. Not only is the Cosmic Disturbance paralleled in the Book of Joel and the Book of Matthew, but the Matthew passage gives us an additional piece of important information, which is, that at the time of The Cosmic Disturbance, that Jesus will come down from Heaven with great power and great glory to gather His elect. This passage also tells us these events will happen immediately after "the tribulation of those days" (Mt. 24:29).

Matthew 24: 29-31

"29Immediately after the tribulation of those days: 'The sun will be darkened, and the moon will not give its light; the stars will fall from the sky, and the powers of the heavens will be shaken. 30At that time the sign of the Son of Man will appear in heaven, and all the tribes of the earth will mourn. They will see the Son of Man coming on the clouds of heaven, with power and great glory. 31And He will send out His angels

with a loud trumpet call, and they will gather His elect from the four winds, from one end of the heavens to the other."

Now we've identified the parallels found in these passages which are Christ's Second Coming, the gathering of the elect, and God's sending His angels with loud trumpets at the same moment of The Cosmic Disturbance.

Let's go ahead and look at the Scripture parallels found in Paul's Epistle to the Thessalonians.

1 Thessalonians 4:16-17

"16For the Lord Himself will descend from heaven with a loud command, with the voice of an archangel, and with the trumpet of God, and the dead in Christ will be the first to rise. 17After that, we who are alive and remain will be caught up together with them in the clouds to meet the Lord in the air. And so we will always be with the Lord."

In these parallel passages, Paul gives us additional information regarding the Second Coming of Jesus Christ. Here we identify the parallel in verse 1 Th. 4:16: *"...Lord Himself will descend from heaven."* Once a parallel verse or phrase has been properly identified within its correct and proper context, then the additional information can be added to complement the previously-paralleled verse or phrase. In 1 Thessalonians 4:16-17 we can identify the passage parallel — that Jesus *"will descend from heaven with a loud command, with the voice of an archangel, and with the trumpet of God."* The first thing I have identified in this text is that, according to the Holy Spirit's description of The Second Coming of Christ, it will be loud and noisy — not secret or invisible. The second thing we see in these parallel passages is the Second Coming of Christ is going to occur simultaneously with The Bodily Resurrection of the elect. We know this because Paul shares an additional piece of information with us about Christ's Second Coming: *"...and the dead in Christ will be the first to rise"* (1Th. 4:16), and *"...we who are alive and remain will be caught up together with them in the clouds to meet the Lord in the air. And so we will always be with the Lord"* (1Th. 4:16-17). Paul tells us The Rapture and The Bodily Resurrection (1Th. 4:16-17) will occur at the same time as Christ's Second Coming (Mt. 24:29-31). When we connect our previously identified parallel passages, we know The Cosmic Disturbance will include The Rapture (1Th. 4:16; Ac. 2:20), Christ's Second Coming (Mt.24:30), and The Bodily Resurrection at the sixth Seal (Rev. 6:12).

Because of the parallel passages identified in Scripture, we know The Cosmic Disturbance will occur at the sixth Seal (Rev. 6:12) and will occur before The Great Day of the Lord (Joel 2:30-32) but after The Great Tribulation (Mt. 24:29) — not before. Paul tells us on the day of Jesus' return, His return will be a noisy and loud event occurring simultaneously with The Bodily Resurrection of the elect (1Th. 4:16-17). These events will occur at the same moment, and then we believers will be with Jesus always (1Th. 4:17).

Now in Revelation 6:12-17, The Apostle John reveals to us, that not only does The Cosmic Disturbance occur at the sixth Seal, but through this additional passage parallel, he gives us more information. He adds here that the stars in the sky will fall to the earth like unripe figs, there will be an earthquake, and mountains will be moved from their place. Also, he tells us that the sky will recede like a scroll being rolled up. It is these events that "cut short" The Great Tribulation period for the sake of the elect (Mt. 24:22), prior to The Day of the Lord (Joel 2:31).

Revelation 6:12-17

"12And when I saw the Lamb open the sixth seal, there was a great earthquake, and the sun became black like sackcloth of goat hair, and the whole moon turned blood red, 13and the stars of the sky fell to the earth, like unripe figs dropping from a tree shaken by a great wind. 14The sky receded like a scroll being rolled up, and every mountain and island was moved from its place. 15Then the kings of the earth, the nobles, the commanders, the rich, the mighty, and every slave and free man, hid in the caves and among the rocks of the mountains. 16And they said to the mountains and the rocks, 'Fall on us and hide us from the face of the One seated on the throne, and from the wrath of the Lamb. 17For the great day of Their wrath has come, and who is able to withstand it?'"

Cosmic Disturbance — Sixth Seal — Parallels Overview
CHART 1

THE PARALLELS BEING FOLLOWED BELOW ARE EXACTLY THE SAME CONTEXT IN EACH PASSAGE — IN THIS CASE, THE SUN BEING DARKENED, THE MOON TURNING BLOOD RED, AND THE DAY OF THE LORD. WHEN WE CONNECT THE PARALLEL PASSAGES, THE ADDITIONAL INFORMATION IS THEN REVEALED.

Joel 2:31

*"31The sun will be turned to darkness and the moon to blood **before** the coming of the great and awesome day of the LORD."*

Matthew 24: 29-31

"29Immediately after the tribulation of those days: 'The sun will be darkened, and the moon will not give its light; the stars will fall from the sky, and the powers of the heavens will be shaken.' 30At that time the sign of the Son of Man will appear in heaven, and all the tribes of the earth will mourn. They will see the Son of Man coming on the clouds of heaven, with power and great glory. 31And He will send out His angels with a loud trumpet call, and they will gather His elect from the four winds, from one end of the heavens to the other."

1 Thessalonians 4:16-17

"16For the Lord Himself will descend from heaven with a loud command, with the voice of an archangel, and with the trumpet of God, and the dead in Christ will be the first to rise. 17After that, we who are alive and remain will be caught up together with them in the clouds to meet the Lord in the air. And so we will always be with the Lord."

Revelation 6:12-17

"12And when I saw the Lamb open the sixth seal, there was a great earthquake, and the sun became black like sackcloth of goat hair, and the whole moon turned blood red, 13and the stars of the sky fell to the earth, like unripe figs dropping from a tree shaken by a great wind. 14The sky receded like a scroll being rolled up, and every mountain and island was moved from its place. 15Then the kings of the earth, the nobles, the commanders, the rich, the mighty, and every slave and free man, hid in the caves and among the rocks of the mountains. 16And they said to the mountains and the rocks, 'Fall on us and hide us from the face of the One seated on the throne, and from the wrath of the Lamb. 17For the great day of Their wrath has come, and who is able to withstand it?'"

Mark 13:24-33

"24However, after the tribulation of those days, 'The sun will be darkened, and the moon will not give its light, 25the stars will fall from the sky, and the powers of the heavens will be shaken.' 26Then they will see the Son of Man coming in the clouds with great power and glory. 27And He will send out the angels to gather His elect from the four winds, from the ends of the earth to the ends of heaven. 28Now learn this lesson from the fig tree: As soon as its branches become tender and sprout leaves, you know that summer is near. 29In the same way, when you see these things happening, you know that He is near, right at the door. 30Truly I tell you, this generation will not pass away until all these things have happened. 31Heaven and earth will pass away, but My words will never pass away. 32But as for that day or hour, no one knows, not even the angels in heaven, nor the Son, but only the Father. 33Be on your guard and stay alert! For you do not know when the appointed time will come."

1. Joel 2:31 tells us that <u>The Day of the Lord</u> will occur <u>after</u> the <u>sun turns dark and the moon turns to blood</u>.

2. Matthew 24:29-31 tells us that when <u>the sun turns dark and the moon turns to blood</u> that it will occur immediately <u>after the tribulation</u> and that the "<u>stars will fall from the sky</u>" and the <u>heavens will be shaken</u>. "The <u>Son of Man will appear in heaven</u>"..."<u>coming on the clouds of heaven, with power and great glory</u>," and <u>His angels will gather His elect</u>.

3. 1 Thessalonians 4:16-17 tells us "<u>the Lord Himself will descend from heaven</u>" and "<u>the dead in Christ will rise first</u>" and <u>those who are alive</u> "<u>will be caught up together with them in the clouds to meet the Lord in the air. And so we will always be with the Lord</u>."

4. Revelation 6:12-17 tells us that when <u>the sun is darkened</u> and <u>the moon is turned blood red</u> this event will occur on the sixth Seal, and there will be <u>an earthquake, all the mountains and islands will be moved from their place, the sky will be rolled up like a scroll</u> and that it is <u>God Who is responsible</u> for <u>cutting short The Great Tribulation for the elect's sake</u> through these <u>cosmic disturbances</u>.

5. Mark 13:24-33 tells us that when the <u>sun turns dark</u> and <u>the moon loses its light</u> and <u>the stars fall from the sky</u>, and <u>the heavens are shaken</u>, then "<u>they will see the Son of Man coming in the clouds with great power and glory. And He will send out the angels to gather His elect....</u>" When you see all these things happening, the end is near. <u>Stay alert</u>.

Cosmic Disturbance — 6th Seal — Parallels Overview CHART 2

THE PARALLELS BEING FOLLOWED BELOW ARE EXACTLY THE SAME CONTEXT IN EACH PASSAGE – IN THIS CASE, THE SUN'S BEING DARKENED, THE MOON'S TURNING BLOOD RED, AND THE DAY OF THE LORD. WHEN WE CONNECT THE PARALLEL PASSAGES, THE ADDITIONAL INFORMATION IS THEN REVEALED.

Isaiah 13:9-11

"9Behold, the Day of the LORD is coming — cruel, with fury and burning anger — to make the earth a desolation and to destroy the sinners within it. 10For the stars of heaven and their constellations will not give their light. The sun will be darkened when it rises, and the moon will not give its light. 11I will punish the world for its evil, and the wicked for their iniquity."

Ezekiel 32:7-9

"7'When I extinguish you, I will cover the heavens and darken their stars. I will cover the sun with a cloud, and the moon will not give its light. 8All the shining lights in the heavens I will darken over you, and I will bring darkness upon your land,' declares the Lord GOD. 9'I will trouble the hearts of many peoples, when I bring about your destruction among the nations, in countries you do not know."

Acts 2:19-21

"19'I will show wonders in the heavens above and signs on the earth below, blood and fire and clouds of smoke. 20The sun will be turned to darkness, and the moon to blood, before the coming of the great and glorious day of the Lord. 21And everyone who calls on the name of the Lord will be saved.'"

Luke 21:25-28

"25There will be signs in the sun and moon and stars, and on the earth dismay among the nations, bewildered by the roaring of the sea and the surging of the waves. 26Men will faint from fear and anxiety over what is coming upon the earth, for the powers of the heavens will be shaken. 27At that time they will see the Son of Man coming in a cloud with power and great glory. 28When these things begin to happen, stand up and lift up your heads, because your redemption is drawing near."

Joel 3:14-16

"14Multitudes, multitudes in the valley of decision! For the Day of the LORD is near in the valley of decision. 15The sun and moon grow dark, and the stars no longer shine. 16The LORD will roar from Zion and raise His voice from Jerusalem; heaven and earth will tremble. But the LORD will be a refuge for His people, a stronghold for the people of Israel."

1. Isaiah 13:9-11 tells us "the Day of the Lord is coming" with cruel "fury and burning anger — to make the earth" desolate "and to destroy the sinners within it...the stars of heaven and their constellations will not give their light. The...sun will be darkened, and the moon will not give its light. [God] will punish the world for its evil and the wicked for their iniquity."

2. Ezekiel 32:7-9 tells us God "will cover the heavens and darken their stars." He "will cover the sun with a cloud, and the moon will not give its light. All the shining lights in the heavens I will darken over you, and I will bring darkness upon your land,' declares the Lord GOD." God "will trouble the hearts of many peoples...."

3. Acts 2:19-21 tells us God "will show wonders in the heavens above and signs on the earth below." There will be blood and fire and clouds of smoke. "The sun will be turned to darkness, and the moon to blood, before the coming of the great and glorious Day of the Lord. And everyone who calls on the name of the Lord will be saved."

4. Luke 21:25-28 tells us that "There will be signs in the sun and moon and stars, and on the earth dismay among the nations, bewildered by the roaring of the sea and the surging of the waves. Men will faint from fear and anxiety over what is coming upon the earth, for the powers of the heavens will be shaken. At that time they will see the Son of Man coming in a cloud with power and great glory. When these things begin to happen, stand up and lift up your heads, because your redemption is drawing near."

5. Joel 3:14-16 tells us that "...the Day of the LORD is near in the valley of decision. The sun and moon will grow dark, and the stars will no longer shine. The LORD will roar from Zion and raise His voice from Jerusalem; heaven and earth will tremble. But the LORD will be a refuge for His people, a stronghold for the people of Israel."

EVENTS ASSOCIATED WITH THE SIXTH SEAL

The Sign & the Pre-Wrath Rapture

Cosmic
Disturbance

MIDPOINT

| Beginning of Sorrows | Great Tribulation | The Day of the Lord |

3-1/2 YEARS   3-1/2 YEARS

anti-Christ Signs
Covenant

Abomination
of Desolation

The Great Tribulation will be cut short for the sake of the elect through these events:
1. Cosmic Disturbance **2.** Earthquake **3.** Mountains Moved **4.** Jesus' Return
5. Saints Resurrected **6.** The Rapture of the Saints **7.** 144,000 Sealed
Prior to the Day of the Lord!

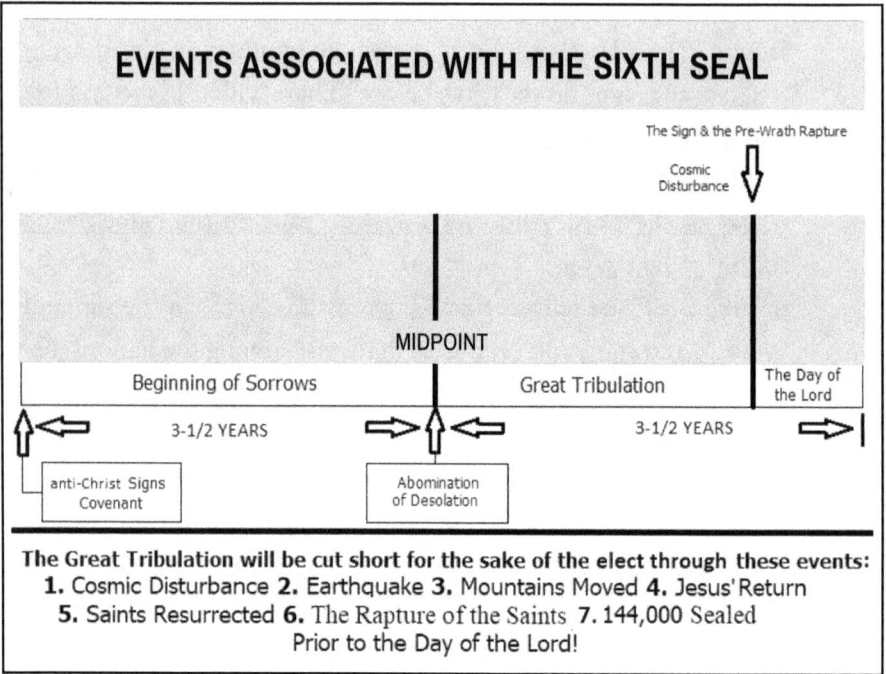

The first five Seals represent The Apostasy, the sixth Seal represents The Cosmic Disturbance that causes The Great Tribulation to be cut short for the sake of the elect and announces the beginning of The Day of the Lord. The seventh Seal represents The Day of the Lord (i.e. God's Wrath).

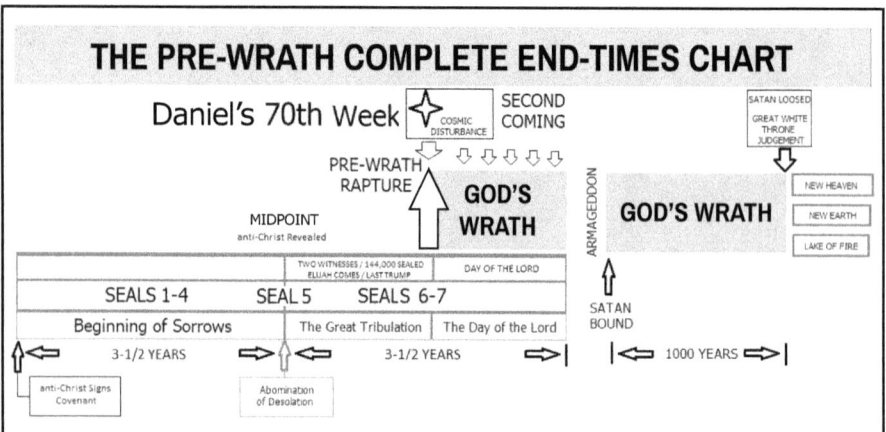

THE PRE-WRATH COMPLETE END-TIMES CHART

Daniel's 70th Week

COSMIC
DISTURBANCE

SECOND
COMING

SATAN LOOSED

GREAT WHITE
THRONE
JUDGEMENT

PRE-WRATH
RAPTURE

**GOD'S
WRATH**

ARMAGEDDON

GOD'S WRATH

NEW HEAVEN

NEW EARTH

LAKE OF FIRE

MIDPOINT
anti-Christ Revealed

TWO WITNESSES / 144,000 SEALED
ELIJAH COMES / LAST TRUMP

DAY OF THE LORD

| SEALS 1-4 | SEAL 5 | SEALS 6-7 |

| Beginning of Sorrows | The Great Tribulation | The Day of the Lord |

SATAN
BOUND

3-1/2 YEARS   3-1/2 YEARS   1000 YEARS

anti-Christ Signs
Covenant

Abomination
of Desolation

Chapter 9

The Great Tribulation and the Day of the Lord

In this chapter I want to explain the Great Tribulation parallels, but I do not want to confuse the Great Tribulation passages with the Day of the Lord passages. There is a distinction made in Scripture between them. According to Daniel 9 and the Revelation 6, the Beginning of Sorrows/Birth Pains and the Great Tribulation are identified as Seals 1-6, and the Day of the Lord is identified as Seal 7, just after the sixth Seal's Cosmic Disturbance. The Prophet Daniel reveals a future event described as The Time of Trouble in Daniel 12:1, and in Jeremiah 30:7 the Prophet Jeremiah talks about a day in the future called Jacob's Distress. He described it as being a time of great fear and trouble and as being like pains of childbirth, and such a time of terror as has never before been in all of history. In similar terms that Jeremiah used, Jesus describes the tribulation as a great time of distress and like birth pains.

Jesus mentions in His Olivet Discourse in Matthew 24:21-22 that the Great Tribulation will occur at the End of the Age and reveals to us that if those days were not cut short, not any flesh would survive on Earth. I am absolutely sure that Jesus, Daniel, and Jeremiah are all describing the same Great Tribulation event.

Matthew 24:21-22

> *"21For at that time there will be great tribulation, unmatched from the beginning of the world until now, and never to be seen again. 22If those days had not been cut short, nobody would be saved. But for the sake of the elect, those days will be shortened."*

I want to discuss with you the importance of accurate Biblical interpretation through the tool identified as "context." In order to use context correctly, we need to understand the circumstances or historical facts that surround a particular event mentioned in Scripture. We need to understand the who, what, why, when, where, and how of the passage in order to determine its correct context. That is why it is so helpful to study passage parallels and read the whole chapter surrounding the specific passage in question. From my experience, I believe this is the best way to determine the correct context of a particular passage. If we do not understand context in the Bible, then we will not be able to make distinctions within Scripture as a whole. For example, we would have a very difficult time making a distinction between passages that apply to the Great Tribulation and the Wrath of God. See the chart below for examples.

Distinguishing Between the Great Tribulation and the Day of the Lord

	Great Tribulation		Day of the Lord
Rev 12:12,17	Satan's wrath against Christians and Jews	Isa 13:11	God's wrath against sinners
Matt 24:21-22; 2 Thess 1:6-7; Rev 6:9-11, 12:17, 13:7, 10	Christians persecuted	Matt 24:29-31, 40-41; 2 Thess 1:6-7; Rev 7:9, 14:14-16	Christians delivered
1 Thess 5:3	People saying "peace and safety"	1 Thess 5:3; Rev 9:6	People under destruction, seeking death but not finding it
Luke 17:27-28	Followers of the man of lawlessness living life as normal	Isa 13:6-8; Zeph 1:11, 13	Followers of the man of lawlessness living in terror, anguish, trouble, and ruin
Rev 13:16-17; Luke 17:28	World economic system set up, people continue buying and selling	Eze 7:19; Zeph 1:11, 13	Wealth of the nations plundered and money is thrown to the ground as worthless
Luke 17:28	People build buildings	Zeph 1:13	Buildings are torn down
Matt 24:15, 21	Man of lawlessness being revealed marks the beginning of this period	Matt 24:19-30; Joel 2:30-32; Isa 13:9-10; Rev 6:12-17	Signs in the heavens and every eye seeing Jesus coming with the clouds marks the start of this period
Rev 13:8	The anti-Christ will set up his kingdom all over the earth. The inhabitants of the earth will follow him.	Zeph 1:18	Earth and people on the earth destroyed
Rev 13:4-5	Man of lawlessness exalted	Isa 2:11, 17	God alone is exalted
2 Thess 2:7	Sin unrestrained	Isa 13:11	Sin punished
Rev 13:4-6	Human arrogance and pride at all-time high	Isa 2:17	Human arrogance and pride brought low
Rev 13:14-15	Idols set up	Isa 2:18, 20	Idols destroyed
Rev 6:9-11; Rev 14:9-10	God's wrath is a yet future event	Rev 6:17; Rev 14:17-19	God's wrath has come
Dan 7:25	Man of lawlessness blasphemes God, persecutes the people of God, and exercises his authority for 3 ½ years.	Dan 7:26; Eze 38:18-23; Rev 16:16-21	God judges the man of lawlessness, revokes his authority, and completely destroys him.

	The Great Tribulation	The Rapture	The Day of the Lord
Days of Noah	Noah lived amongst a violent people who were living unconcerned and unprepared for God's judgment.	Noah and his family boarded the ark before God poured out his judgment on the world.	While Noah and his family floated safely above the waters, the flood destroyed the world at that time.
Days of Lot	Lot lived amongst a perverse, arrogant people who were unconcerned and unprepared for God's judgment.	Lot and his family fled to a nearby city before God poured out his judgment on Sodom and Gomorrah and the surrounding towns.	While Lot and his daughters were safe in a nearby city, burning sulfur rained down from heaven and destroyed Sodom.
Generation Before Jesus Returns	Christians will live during the worst generation in the history of mankind that willfully rejects God and worships satan and the anti-Christ.	Jesus returns on the clouds and catches Christians up into the sky to be with him before the Day of the Lord.	Christians will be rewarded in heaven, have new resurrected bodies, and will enjoy the wedding feast while God pours out destruction on the earth.

The chart above shows the parallels in the lives of Noah and Lot relative to the Great Tribulation, the Rapture, and the Day of the Lord. What amazes me is the current condition of our generation in 2023 is easily a mirrored image of the condition of Noah's and Lot's generations. If God does not judge this generation for their sin, then He owes Noah's and Lot's generation an apology.

Jesus told His disciples in Matthew 24:37-39 that the End Times would be like those during the days of Noah.

Matthew 24:37-39

"*37As it was in the days of Noah, so will it be at the coming of the Son of Man. 38For in the days before the flood, people were eating and drinking, marrying and giving in marriage, up to the day Noah entered the ark. 39And they were oblivious, until the flood came and swept them all away. So will it be at the coming of the Son of Man.*"

It appears people thought they were living normal lives during the time of Noah, just before the flood. They were oblivious to the impending disaster — just like our generation today!

The Apostle Paul said, before Christ's return, the world would have perilous times filled with pleasure-seeking, materialism, immorality, violence, idleness, and a rejection of the things of God (2Tim. 3:1-5). I think we need to ask ourselves at least this one question: What were the conditions in

Noah's day that warranted God's judgment, and why should we be concerned? One of many major reasons for why God brought judgment upon the world through the Great Flood was that the earth was filled with violence (Ge. 6:13). Surprisingly, in today's modern culture there has been an alarming increase in global violence just in the past 100 years. Wars in the past 90 years have killed more people than the previous 500 years combined.[3] An estimated 203 million people were killed by wars just in the Twentieth Century.[4]

Between 170 and 360 million people were killed by governments in the Twentieth Century, apart from war. Recently, more civilians have been killed in armed conflicts than the combatants themselves, accounting for 90 percent of casualties since 1942. Just in the last decade, war has claimed the lives of an estimated two million children and has disabled another four to five million children. There is also a silent form of violence that is being perpetrated around the world by the deliberate act of abortions (i.e. murder) of innocent children. Each year globally about 73 million abortions are performed.[5] Indeed, the people of this world are exactly the way Jesus described them. Jesus Christ said in Matthew 15:19, *"¹⁹For out of the heart come evil thoughts, murder, adultery, sexual immorality, theft, false testimony, and slander."* Studies have shown that just in the United States alone a typical child will view more than 200,000 acts of violence, including 16,000 murders, on television before the age of 18. Television programs display approximately 812 acts of violence per hour. Another form of exposure to violence is accessed on the internet and video games. As violence of this age increases, God's message becomes more fitting. We read about this in the Holy Bible by the Prophet Hosea:

Hosea 4:1-3

> *"¹Hear the word of the LORD, O children of Israel, for the LORD has a case against the people of the land: 'There is no truth, no loving devotion, and no knowledge of God in the land! ²Cursing and lying, murder and stealing, and adultery are rampant; one act of bloodshed follows another. ³Therefore the land mourns, and all who dwell in it will waste*

---

3   https://www.worldrevolution.org
4   Matthew White, Historical Atlas of the Twentieth Century, 2010, ("Deaths by War").
5   Abortions globally. Source: www.who.int/news-room/fact-sheets/detail/abortion; https://www.guttmacher.org/fact-sheet/induced-abortion-worldwide; https://www.pewresearch.org/short-reads/2023/01/11/what-the-data-says-about-abortion-in-the-u-s-2/.

away with the beasts of the field and the birds of the air; even the fish of the sea disappear.'"

The Man of Lawlessness Chart parallels the 70th Week of Daniel, 2 Thessalonians, and The Book of Revelation.

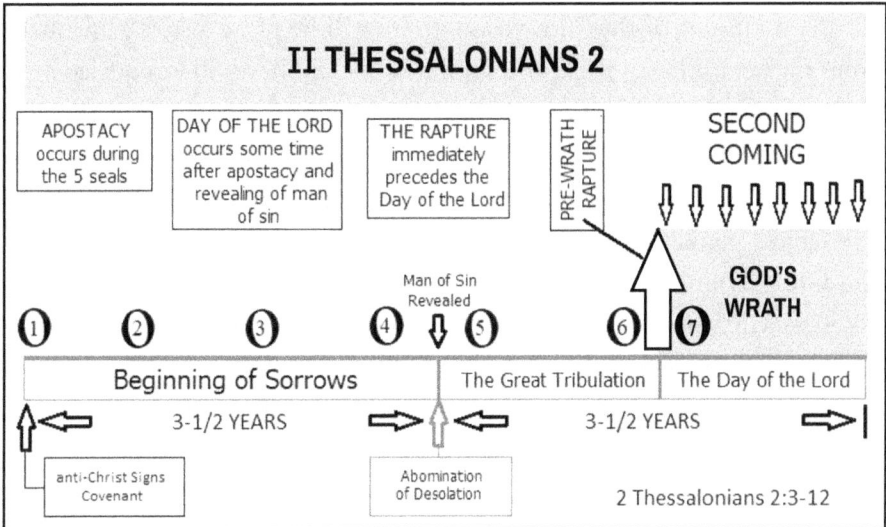

The numbers 1–7 above represent the seven Seals which include the seven Trumpets and seven Bowls found within the Scroll itself. The contents of the Scroll is God's judgments revealed once the seven Seals have been removed.

The ant-Christ has many titles equated to him such as these:

- Man of Sin
- Man of Lawlessness
- Man of Rebellion
- Man of Insurrection
- Man of Apostasy

The man of lawlessness will appear suddenly (2Th. 2:3). He is doomed for destruction (2Th. 2:8). He will operate in deception (2Th. 2:9-10). He will oppose God (2Th. 2:4). He is held back by either the Holy Spirit or Michael the Archangel (2Th. 2:6-7; Da. 12:1; Rev. 12:6-8). The answer to this last statement will be completely contingent upon the Rapture position that you currently follow. I believe the restrainer is Michael the archangel (2Th. 2:6-8), and I want to explain why. Those who embrace the view of a

Pre-Tribulation Rapture, or even a Mid-Tribulation Rapture view, believe that the "restrainer" is the Holy Spirit because they will argue that once the Christian Church is caught-up at the Rapture, the Holy Spirit will also be removed from the earth, and this removal would enable the anti-Christ to quickly rise to power. Jesus indicated that following the abomination of desolation (at the midpoint of the 70th week), there will be great distress, unequaled from the beginning of the world until now — and never to be equaled again (Mt. 24: 21). The Old Testament prophet Daniel indicated that just prior to this same time period of distress, the archangel Michael would "arise" (Da. 12:1). The archangel Michael always has been the special protective "prince" of Daniel's people, Israel (Da. 10:13). Let me explain. At the beginning of the Great Tribulation or at the midpoint of the 70th week, the archangel Michael will "arise" or "stand-up." This term used in the Hebrew is the word *amad*, which actually means to "stand aside," "stand still," "desist," or be "inactive." Other examples of the usage of the Hebrew word *amad* are found in Job 32:16, Nehemiah 8:5, and 2 Samuel 18:30. The reason why I do not believe the restrainer is, in fact, the Holy Spirit is that, from a Pre-Wrath Rapture view perspective, the Rapture of the Church does not occur until the sixth Seal is opened, and the Scripture teaches us that the Holy Spirit lives inside the followers of Christ forever. Christ told His followers, "...surely I am with you always, even to the end of the age." (Mt. 28:20). Jesus tells us in John 14:16-17 that the Holy Spirit will be with us forever. We read, *"¹⁶And I will ask the Father, and He will give you another Advocate to be with you forever — ¹⁷the Spirit of truth. The world cannot receive Him, because it neither sees Him nor knows Him. But you do know Him, for He abides with you and will be in you."* This is why I believe the "restrainer" is Michael the archangel — because if the Christian Church is on the earth until the sixth Seal is broken, then so is the Holy Spirit! What this means is if you hold to a Pre-Tribulation position, or even a Mid-Tribulation position, then you are logically forced to believe that the Holy Spirit is the "restrainer;" but if you hold to the Pre-Wrath Rapture position, then you would logically have to abide by what The Holy Scriptures actually teach. Also, if the Holy Spirit is the restraining force that is removed, then what need is there for the Two Witnesses, and how could they accomplish God's Work in the Great Tribulation period without the Holy Spirit (Rev. 11:3-11), and how could the 144,000 Jews sealed by God (Rev. 7:4) evangelize the post-rapture world and proclaim the Gospel during the Great Tribulation period (Rev. 7:9)? Many will come to faith in Christ through their ministering during the 70th Week of Daniel. How could either of these End Time ministries achieve God's goals without the Work of the Holy Spirit?

Chapter 10

The 70th-Week Hypothesis

Again I want to remind you that this is a WORD to the watchful, and a WARNING to the wayward! It is my educated and well-researched opinion that we could possibly be in the 70th Week of Daniel in the month of September, in the year of our Lord Jesus Christ 2023. Because I am so sure that my opinion is correct, I am willing to put my reputation out on a limb in order to alert the Body of Christ of the potential possibility of this opinion. I want to explain the reasoning behind this opinion, and you decide its plausibility. I want to point out to you, that I am not a fan — or ever have been in my life — of interpreting Biblical prophecy by reading a newspaper or through observing current events. This method of interpreting Scripture is called *eisegesis*. For those who do not know, this method occurs when the interpreter reads something into the text that is not originally in the text, and this method is not a healthy and well-balanced approach to the Biblical interpretation of Scripture, to say the least. I will be implementing an exegesis method of interpretation, which means that I will draw out of the text something that is originally in the text by using Scripture itself. That's why I use the hermeneutical method of exegesis study identified as passage paralleling. Let me explain. Daniel 9:27 tells us that the beginning of The 70th Week will start when the anti-Christ signs a seven-year agreement with Israel and with the many.

Daniel 9:27

> *"27And he will confirm a covenant with many for one week, but in the middle of the week he will put an end to sacrifice and offering. And on the wing of the temple will come the abomination that causes desolation, until the decreed destruction is poured out upon him."*

It is also my educated and well-researched opinion that the United Nations Environmental Program of 1972, and the United Nations Agenda 21 of 1992, were just dress rehearsals for the current unprecedented and aggressive seven-year Agenda 30 of 2023. The 17 Sustainable Development Goals (SDG7) were adopted by the United Nations in 2015 as "a universal call to action to end poverty, protect the planet, and ensure that by 2030 all people enjoy Peace and Prosperity."[6] It is my opinion that Agenda 30 SDG7 could be the actual seven-year agreement between the Nation of Israel, the unrevealed anti-Christ, and the many, as mentioned by the Prophet Daniel in Daniel 9:24-27.

The United Nations' aggressive Agenda 30 (i.e. SDG7) is the seven-year mighty and firm agreement the Prophet Daniel spoke about that will be made between The Nation of Israel, the anti-Christ, and the many which fits perfectly with the Agenda 30's 17 Sustainable Development Goals. When we go to the United Nations website,[7] we can read about this seven-year agreement with the Nation of Israel and the many (i.e. the 193 United Nations member states). It is an aggressive agreement for the next seven years (2023-2030), having started in the month of September18-19, 2023 (or effective start date). There are approximately 193 United Nations member states that have all agreed to try to achieve the Agenda 30's 17 Sustainable Development Goals by the year 2030. Below is a list of the 193 United Nations Sustainable Development Goals signees (i.e. the many). Israel is also a member state of the United Nations and has signed the agreement with the United Nations.

---

6   https://www.un.org/sustainabledevelopment/development-agenda.

7   United Nations SDG7 World Bank Group and the 2030 Agenda https://www.worldbank.org., and Sustainable Development Goals – https://sdgs.un.org/goals. United Nations Development Program https://www.undp.org. Population Matters – https://www.unfpa.org. United Nation Environment Program – https://www.unep.org.

After researching information on the SDG7 website, I found out all member countries are responsible for their own individual country's Agenda 30 goals and successes — which means that every member country will not only be responsible for funding Agenda 30 but also be responsible for its own country's enforcement, which will includes its own police and military departments. The SDG7 rules will also apply to the United States of America as well because the U.S. is also a member state and will be required to follow the same rules as the rest of the member states who signed the agreement. All 193 United Nations member countries signed on to the 17 Sustainable Development Goals (SDG7) "to create a future we want in 2030."[8]

Afghanistan	Colombia	Guyana	Mauritania
Albania	Comoros	Haiti	Mauritius
Algeria	Congo	Honduras	Mexico
Andorra	Costa Rica	Hungry	Micronesia
Angola	Côte d'Ivoire	Iceland	Monaco
Antigua and Barbuda	Croatia	India	Mongolia
Argentina	Cuba	Indonesia	Montenegro
Armenia	Cyprus	Iran	Morocco
Australia	Czechia	Iraq	Mozambique
Austria	D. P. Republic of Korea	Ireland	Myanmar
Azerbaijan	D.P. of the Congo	Israel	Namibia
Bahamas	Denmark	Italy	Nauru
Bahrain	Djibouti	Jamaica	Nepal
Bangladesh	Dominica	Japan	Netherlands
Barbados	Dominican Republic	Jordan	New Zealand
Belarus	Ecuador	Kazakhstan	Nicaragua
Belgium	Egypt	Kenya	Niger
Belize	El Salvador	Kiribati	Nigeria
Benin	Equatorial Guinea	Kuwait	North Macedonia
Bhutan	Eritrea	Kyrgyzstan	Norway
Bolivia	Estonia	Lao People's Republic	Oman
Bosnia and Herzegovina	Eswatini	Latvia	Pakistan
Botswana	Ethiopia	Lebanon	Palau
Brazil	Fiji	Lesotho	Panama
Brunei Darussalam	Finland	Liberia	Papua New Guinea
Bulgaria	France	Libya	Paraguay
Burkina Faso	Gabon	Liechtenstein	Peru
Burundi	Gambia	Lithuania	Philippines
Cabo Verde	Georgia	Luxembourg	Poland
Cambodia	Germany	Madagascar	Portugal
Cameroon	Ghana	Malawi	Qatar
Canada	Greece	Malaysia	Republic of Korea
Central African Republic	Grenada	Maldives	Republic of Moldova
Chad	Guatemala	Mali	Romania
Chile	Guinea	Malta	Russian Federation
China	Guinea Bissau	Marshall Island	Rwanda

Samoa	Slovenia	Tajikistan	United Kingdom of Great Britain and Northern Ireland
San Marino	Solomon Islands	Thailand	United Republic of Tanzania
Sao Tome and Principe	Somalia	Timor-Leste	United States of America
Saint Kitts and Nevis	South Africa	Togo	Uruguay
Saint Vincent and the Grenadines	South Sudan	Tonga	Uzbekistan
Saudi Arabia	Spain	Trinidad and Tobago	Venezuela, Republic of Bolivarian
Senegal	Sri Lanka	Tunisia	Viet Nam
Serbia	Sudan	Turkey	Yemen
Seychelles	Switzerland	Turkmenistan	Zambia
Sierra Leone	Syrian Arab Republic	Tuvalu	Zimbabwe
Singapore	Suriname	Uganda Ukraine	
Slovakia	Sweden	United Arab Emirates	

All the 193 United Nation member states have agreed to attempt to achieve the 17 Sustainable Development Goals of Agenda 30 by the year 2030 — including the Nation of Israel and the United States of America. I believe that this SDG7 aggressive seven-year agreement began at the Agenda 30 Summit on September 18-19, 2023 (or its effective start date). What got my attention was that I had never seen such organized globalization before, with so many world leaders around the globe who made pledges and plans and implemented a call-to-action across such a broad and universal commitment for Agenda 30 goals and policies. The world is united together for the very first time in my 62 years of living. Devoted to saving the world and all of humanity from themselves, the world is on a path of Sustainable Development Goals to do so. This is an unprecedented global agenda. I must be honest with you: I did not see this one coming! It did catch me by surprise. When I started my investigation of Agenda 30, I needed to know more details of the SDG7 agreement. Specifically, I needed to know what exactly signing the Sustainable Development Goal agreement means for each individual U.N. member state. What are each U.N. member state's responsibilities in the SDG7 agreement? One of the major reasons that I needed to know about each member state's responsibilities is that two of the member states that have signed the SDG7 agreement are the United States of America and the Nation of Israel. I went to the Sustainable Development Goals website where I found my answers. First, I want to show you below the list of the actual 17 SDG7 goals that are also accompanied by 169 specific targets and 232 measurable indicators to help countries plan their progress, find gaps and report the results to the international communities that I found on the U.N. website. The 17 Sustainable Development Goals (SDG) that all 193 United Nations member states have agreed upon are listed on the following page.

The 17 Sustainable Development Goals:
1. No Poverty
2. Zero Hunger
3. Good Health and Well-Being
4. Quality Education
5. Gender Equality
6. Clean Water
7. Affordable and Clean Energy
8. Decent Work and Economic Growth
9. Industry, Innovation, and Infrastructure
10. Reduced Inequalities
11. Sustainable Cities and Communities
12. Responsible Consumption and Production
13. Climate Action
14. Life Below Water
15. Life On Land
16. Peace, Justice, and Strong Institutions
17. Partnership for the Goals

These 17 Sustainable Development Goals mentioned above sound too good to be true, and for good reason, because they are, in fact, too good to be true. The United Nations portrays itself as being helpful, concerned, and doing what is beneficial and caring for both humanity and Earth. These Agenda 30 goals give the impression that the United Nations is rescuing or saving us and the planet from ourselves. This would imply, from my Biblical perspective, that the anti-Christ, in the beginning 3-1/2 years of Daniel's 70th Week, is working through the United Nations and is acting like a type of savior, or a type of Christ (i.e. false Christ) — I reiterate — *in the beginning.* This is exactly the first thing that Christ and The Apostle John said would happen at the beginning of The Birth Pains. Let me explain. When we parallel the Olivet Discourse Prophecies, Jesus tells us that there will be false Christ's (Mt. 24:24) that will come to deceive many. Could the 193 plus more U.N. member states' agreeing to the 17 SDG7 goals that would rescue humanity and save the planet be what Christ, to a certain extent, meant by false Christ's (i.e. false saviors)? Could the United Nation Assembly be the platform that will be used by the anti-Christ to conquer through diplomacy, not a sword, until the "restrainer" is removed? Could this also be what is spoken of in the Apostle John's vision about a rider on a white horse in Revelation 6:1-2 who rode out as a conqueror focused on conquering, wearing a crown, and carrying a bow without arrows? John does not mention that this rider has any arrows. According to some Bible teachers, the rider of this white horse who carries a bow with no arrows is mistakenly identified as Jesus Christ. The reason we know this rider is not Jesus Christ is that he then proceeds to sign a covenant with Israel and the many and then later backs out of the seven-year agreement with Israel in 3-1/2 years and causes the Abomination of Desolation in the new Temple, and after that, proceeds to kill Jews and Christians. Do these characteristics really sound like they accurately describe the characteristics of the Son of God, Jesus Christ, as He is portrayed in the Scriptures? The rider on the white horse of Revelation 6:1-2 is clearly mimicking the True Christ mentioned in Revelation 19:11. When Jesus Christ comes back on a white horse, He will have many crowns (Rev 19:12) and be carrying a sword with the intent to bring justice to the world. The rider of the white horse in Revelation 6:1-2 is clearly not Jesus Christ described in Revelation 19:11 but is a false Christ mentioned by Jesus Christ Himself in His Olivet Discourse Prophecies. I believe the rider on the white horse that John prophesied about in Revelation 6:1-2 is the anti-Christ, and this rider on the white horse in Revelation 6:1-2 will seek to be worshipped. He will have a false religion around him. Because John mentions that the rider is carrying a bow but does not mention that the rider has any arrows, and John tells us the rider is wearing a crown and riding a white horse, many Biblical Greek scholars tell us that these descriptions could be symbolic of a political and economic power, which will fight a battle without swords and sheds no blood in the beginning. Many scholars refer to the rider on the white horse in Revelation 6:1-2 as a peaceful conqueror because he has a bow with no arrows. Usually a bow in the hand represents a symbol of aggressive warfare; but — I emphasize — John tells us this rider is on a white horse, with a crown, but does not say the rider has any arrows. This clearly means, according to many Bible scholars, that he will conquer by diplomacy — not war. This is exactly what we see with the SDG7 agreement. He will usher in a false peace and will be extremely popular with the masses, in the beginning. The world will think that he will solve all the world's problems. He will be able to extend his influence with words of diplomacy. He will be hailed as a hero in the beginning. The fact that he was given a crown shows he will be successful, as people fall in line with his leadership, as he rules the world. The fact that he was given a crown also means he was given authority to rule. I think these above-mentioned descriptions are symbolic of a conqueror who overcomes by simply urging or convincing his enemies with words, intellect, and reason — to make peace while there is still time. The symbolism associated with this description — the rider on the white horse, holding a bow without arrows, wearing a crown — is absolutely consistent with the 17 United Nations 2030 Agenda Goals. The United Nations has been given authority. They are victorious with power (i.e. wearing a crown) in conquering the world with a bow with no arrows. These above interpretations of the Revelation 6:1-2 Bible passages are completely consistent with what I read on the SDG7 website. Let me explain. I went to the Sustainable Development Goals websites and found many alarming quotes there. Just a few samples of what I found[9] are as follows:

> "All of us will work to implement the Agenda within our own countries and at the regional and global levels."

> "The scale and ambition of the Agenda requires a revitalized global partnership to ensure its implantation. We fully commit to this…."

> "It will facilitate an intensive global engagement of all in support of implementation of all the goals and targets, bringing together Governments, the Private sector, civil society, the United Nations System and other actors and mobilizing all available resources."

> "All countries and all stakeholders, acting in collaborative partnership, will implement this plan. We are resolved to free the human race from the tyranny of poverty…."

---

9   Sustainable Development Goals (http://www.sdgs.un.org/goals)

"We are determined to take the bold transformative steps which are urgently needed to shift the world into a sustainable and resilient path."

"We are committed to achieving Sustainable Development in its three dimensions — economics, social and environmental — in a balanced and integrated manner."

"This is an Agenda of unprecedented scope and significance. It is accepted by all Countries..."

"Never before have world leaders pledged common action and endeavor across such a broad and universal policy agenda. We are setting out together on the path toward sustainable development, devoting ourselves collectively to pursuit of global development and of 'win-win' cooperation which can bring huge gains to all countries and all parts of the world."

Also, the World Health Organization, along with many other organizations are supporting and implementing the Sustainable Development Goals (SDG).[10] The World Health Organization announced "that all United Nation members may become members of WHO by accepting its constitution. Other countries may become members when their application has been approved by a simple majority vote of the World Health Assembly. Despite its failure during COVID-19 and complicity in China's cover-up, the World Health Organization (WHO) in 2023 has drafted a new global pandemic treaty entitled, *The WHO Pandemic Preparedness Treaty*.[11] The draft treaty focuses on expanding WHO power, trampling intellectual property rights, and "equitably" redistributing knowledge, technology, and other resources. The U.S. has historically been one of the largest funders of WHO, providing between $200 million and $600 million annually over the last decade. In 2020, the Trump administration suspended financial support and initiated a process to withdraw the U.S. from membership in the organization, but Biden reversed that decision upon taking office in January 2021 and restored U.S. funding to WHO.

---

10 The World Health Organization, the United Nations agency working to promote health, keep the world safe and serve the vulnerable. https://www.who.int

11 https://www.weforum.org/agenda/2023/05/who-pandemic-treaty-what-how-work/. https://www.who.int/newsroom/question-and-answers/item/pandemic-prevention-preparedness-and-response-accord.

Also, the BRICS countries[12] have a huge potential role in achieving the 17 Agenda 2030 goals.[13] Brazil, Russia, India, China, and South Africa have five of the world's most important emerging economies. They are key players to the success of the 2030 Agenda for Sustainable Development. Let me explain. BRICS are members of the G20, they account for 43% of the world's population, and at least 23% of the GDP, and they represent 16% of the world trade. The BRICS countries have become a united force with a strong desire to move forward with their development strategies, which includes the 17 Sustainable Development Goals.[14] All member countries of BRICS together have an amazing level of production and development abilities. For example, Russia has become the largest exporter of wheat; China has the globe's largest industrial and manufacturing capacity; India is the leader of the scientific, technological, and pharmaceutical fields; Brazil is endowed with an abundance of minerals and water and biological and ecological resources; and South Africa abounds in natural resources.

The above details mean that the BRICS countries have positioned themselves to take the leading role in helping to achieve the 2030 Agenda. Also the BRICS countries have developed a BRICS Bank located in Shanghai, China, called *The New Development Bank* (aka — BRICS Development Bank).[15]

Proposed BRICS Expansion

Current BRICS members
Proposed BRICS members

12   BRICS 2023: Home. https://brics2023.gov.za
13   https://sdgs.un.org/goals
14   Agenda 30 17 sustainable goals to improve our world, https://www.globalgoals.org
15   BRICS New Development Bank is a Sustainable Development Bank – https://www.ndb.int/

Over 40 countries, including Saudi Arabia, Iran, United Arab Emirates, Argentina, Indonesia, Egypt, and Ethiopia have expressed interest in joining BRICS, according to South Africa. The admittance of Saudi Arabia into BRICS alone could force the European Union to abandon the U.S. dollar, and then the EU would have to settle their gas and oil trade with a different currency. This would mean that, if Saudi Arabia joined BRICS and they only accept BRICS currency, even just this one action itself would change the United States of America's economic situation.

ATTENTION READER: This just in — Saudi Arabia is now a member on the BRICS Financial Treaty and, in addition to that news, the Saudi Crown Prince Mahammed bin Salman said in a rare interview with Fox News on Wednesday, September 27, 2023, "that negotiations over Israel means the prospects of normalized relations between both countries 'get closer' every day." Also, Israel's Prime Minister Benjamin Netanyahu addressed the 78th Session of the United Nations General Assembly, Friday, September 22, 2023, at the United Nations headquarters saying, "that Israel is 'at a cusp' of a historic agreement with Saudi Arabia." This is very interesting and fits perfectly with The 70th-Week Hypothesis. As more and more countries look to join BRICS, they have added the symbol (+) to their name. Eventually it will be referred to as BRICS+. One of the things that I think will come out of the BRICS governments is the forming of the one-world government. I do believe BRICS will eventually bring into the world a one-world currency and economic system as well. I believe the United Nations will be used by the anti-Christ to achieve his financial globalization agenda. He will need a financial globalization system to be in place so he can regulate and control all the financial transactions of everyone in his one-world economic system. Only people of the world who have his mark on their right hand or their forehead will be able to buy and sell. He will also need to have a technological globalization in order to put his financial system in place. There will be a political globalization in place as well so that he can, through treaties and wars, bring the world under his authority. Also, he will need a cultural and social globalization in place for him to start and maintain his own one-world false religion where his false prophet can operate. He will also need an agricultural globalization in the beginning for taking over the world's food industry with the promise to provide food for everyone. He will have the technology, the power, the money, and the support of the majority of the planet's human population, *in the beginning*. He will also grab all the world's power grids and supplies. He will have all the world's surveillance technologies — including all the satellite and video technologies. He will have control over all the world's computer software technologies. He will have control over all the financial systems and banking institutions globally. I find it amazing that the globalization of the world's technologies that are necessary for the implementation of Bible prophecy in the End of the Age is exactly what is available today in our modern society in 2023. He will be in control of all the world's internet technologies and capabilities, including Jeff Bezos' Project Kuiper, also known as Everywhere Internet (i.e. VLEO G6 Technologies).[16] The FCC has already approved it (i.e. Amazon Internet), and it is going to be launched on December 31, 2023. I believe that it is going to be an incredible internet technology because the founder of Amazon, Jeff Bezos, is currently selling billions of dollars of Amazon stock to invest in what he calls Project Kuiper. The anti-Christ will also have control over all the world's militaries. We know that he will have at least each of the 193 United Nations member state's police and military departments available, including the Nation of Israel's and the United States of America's. For example, if the U.S. is still a world power during that time, he will use all the available organizations and resources available of the U.S. for accomplishing the 17 goals of Agenda 30, and the reason he will be allowed to do this is that the U.S. signed the aggressive seven-year SDG7 agreement and is a SDG7 U.N. member, which will make available all U.S. resources such as the FBI, CIA, FTA, FCC, ATF, Marines, Army, Navy, Air Force, Space Force, DOJ, FEMA, and OSHA — and many more. He will have the full cooperation of organizations outside of the U.S.A. as well, such as WHO, CDC, WEF, and U.N. He will be in control of all the world's food and water supplies. This Agenda 30 cooperation includes all 193 United Nations member state countries and their resources, including all the BRICS nations as well. Think about that for a

---

16 https://www.huawei.com/en/huaweitech/future-technologies/very-low-earth-orbit-satellite-networks-6g7ved

moment. This is real, folks! They all signed the SDG7 Agenda 30 agreement on September 18-19, 2023.

As you can see, the Sustainable Development Goals (SDG7), or Agenda 2030, will create a huge problem for the American population and the United States Constitution as the Agenda 30 SDG7 starts to aggressively implement their goals in our country, as well as many other countries around the world. Obviously, I believe eventually it will somehow supersede the U. S. Constitution and the basic human rights of American citizens because of the possibility of the United States' signing of *The WHO Pandemic Preparedness Treaty.* The 17 SDG7 goals will be self-funded by each state of the U.S. individually, according to the SDG7 agreement. Each U.N. member state is responsible for its own country's SDG7 funding, enforcement, and the 17 goals' implementation — the majority of the U.N. countries of the world, according to their SDG7 agreement, all 193 United Nation members, of which the United States of America is a member, which means the United Nations' SDG7 goals will be aggressively pursued in all these 193 plus nations, including the U.S., in an attempt to achieve the Agenda 2030 — 17 goals within a seven-year period — 2023-2030. This fits perfectly with The 70th Week of Daniel, the Olivet Discourse, and Revelation 6-8. According to the U.N. agreement signed by all the 193 United Nations members, including the United States, this means, according to the Sustainable Development Goals agreement implemented by the U.N. Agenda 2030, the U.N. Agenda 30 SDG7 goals will be funded by American citizens with American tax dollars. These goals will also be funded by the BRICS + countries and the World Health Organization through money obtained by support from global partners. The world has already observed what the WHO organization can achieve through the recent COVID-19 pandemic. They were able to lock down multiple nations and mandate vaccines, testing, and mask-wearing. Their power and influence globally has been very impressive as we witnessed countries around the world complying, such as Canada, France, China, Australia, Argentina, Peru, Chile, South Korea, Sweden, Taiwan, Japan, Hong Kong, and Brazil — and many, many more countries. They were able to implement mandates and enforce the lockdown of schools, universities, colleges, businesses, and churches.

I think the mandates and lockdowns in some of these countries are still in force even today in 2023, and they are probably going to start it all over again because of a new COVID variant that has been identified. The WHO has dispensed vaccines globally to around 73.3 percent of the world population as of 2023. Imagine if all authoritative organizations within a country were able to accomplish a similar success in achieving the 17 SDG's. Also, virtually all the world's largest companies are on board with the SDG and are now issuing a sustainability report. That's more than 2,000 companies that have a scientific-based carbon target, and about one-third of these companies pledge to reach net zero by 2050. Twenty-eight companies with a total market capitalization of 1.3 trillion dollars stepped up to set a new level of climate response to a call-to-action campaign ahead of the United Nation Climate Summit on September 18-19, 2023. On August 22-24, 2023, the 15th BRICS Summit occurred in Johannesburg, South Africa. On September 18-19, 2023, the 2030 Agenda Summit happened in New York. Here are some quotes by the U.N. and Antonio Guterres U.N. Secretary-General:

"The SDG Summit in September must be a moment of unity to provide a renewed impetus and accelerated actions for reaching the SDG's." — Antonio Guterres, United Nations Secretary-General

"The 2030 SDG Summit will mark the beginning of a new phase of accelerated progress towards the Sustainable Development Goals with high-level political guidance on transformative and accelerated actions leading up to 2030." — www.un.org

Based on all the obvious signs that The 70th Week of Daniel could have possibly begun in the month of September 18-19, 2023 (or its effective date), it did not officially start until the official effective date of the agreement between the anti-Christ, Israel, and the many (i.e.193 U.N. member states). This is an exciting time for the believer in Jesus Christ. We will actually see Bible Prophecy unfold before our very eyes — in real time! If my hypothesis is correct, then according to Daniel's 70th Week, Jesus' Olivet Discourse, and John's Scroll and seven Seals from the Book of Revelation, we know the exact sequence of events in their chronological order, which means that, if we survive the entire 70th Week of Daniel which includes the Birth Pains and the Great Tribulation, and make it all the way to the to the sixth Seal of Revelation, we will actually experience the Second Coming of Christ, the Rapture, and the Bodily Resurrection — while still living on Earth. But if we die from war, famine, pestilence, or martyrdom sometime before the sixth Seal, we will begin our new life with Christ sooner rather than later (Ph. 1:21). Hallelujah! Praise the Lord! Get ready, Church. Jesus is coming for us — according to the Holy Bible — somewhere between six or seven years after the start date of the covenant's effective signing date. Get ready, Saints, and for Christ's sake, begin reaching a lost and dying world with the Gospel of Jesus Christ before a lost and dying world's opportunity passes. God has provided us in His Word a blueprint of what is going to take place during Daniel's 70th Week. As we rapidly approach the Second Coming of Jesus Christ, we must understand the meaning of the level of the severity of God's judgment on a lost and dying world, which reveals to us the great cost of Jesus' salvation in sparing us from God's judgment. Once we understand our horrific human condition and the only solution for that horrific human condition as it has been revealed to us through Scripture (1 Tim. 2:5-6), we then can understand the level of the importance of sharing the Gospel with as many lost souls as we possibly can during the last seven years of our current earthly existence. That's why the Holy Bible tells us that "today is the day of salvation" (2Cor. 6:2). The New Testament tells us over 200 times that we must come to God on His terms through Jesus Christ (Jn. 1:12; 3:16-18; Ac. 16:31; Rom. 10:9).

If you are a believer, preparing for the Rapture event is not about fear but it is about our hope and trust in Christ. It is about the commitment that shapes our life, beliefs, and actions — in other words, what we say, do, and think. It is a reminder to live a life centered on Christ — exhibiting love, forgiveness, and righteous living, while earnestly anticipating Christ's Return.

Remember that the God we serve is our strength. He will never leave us or forsake us. He hears our prayers. He gives us forgiveness and salvation. He will give us peace, and He will always love us. Every day will draw us closer to our King's arrival! Hang on to the Holy Spirit through His Holy Word and daily prayer, and never let go of Him!

I came across these statistics in my research for this book in a recent Pew Research Report. The report states that only four in ten U.S. adults believe they are living in the End Times.

A slight majority of Americans believe Jesus will return to Earth one day

Do you believe Jesus will return to Earth someday?

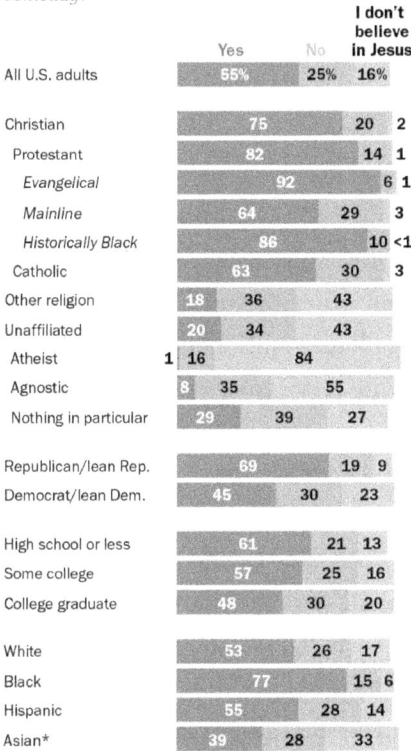

	Yes	No	I don't believe in Jesus
All U.S. adults	55%	25%	16%
Christian	75	20	2
Protestant	82	14	1
Evangelical	92	6	1
Mainline	64	29	3
Historically Black	86	10	<1
Catholic	63	30	3
Other religion	18	36	43
Unaffiliated	20	34	43
Atheist	1	16	84
Agnostic	8	35	55
Nothing in particular	29	39	27
Republican/lean Rep.	69	19	9
Democrat/lean Dem.	45	30	23
High school or less	61	21	13
Some college	57	25	16
College graduate	48	30	20
White	53	26	17
Black	77	15	6
Hispanic	55	28	14
Asian*	39	28	33

*Estimates for Asian adults are representative of English speakers only.
Note: Those who did not answer are not shown. White, Black and Asian adults include those who report being only one race and are not Hispanic. Hispanics are of any race. "Other religion" includes those who identify as Jewish, Muslim, Buddhist, Hindu, or with another world religion or other non-Christian faith.
Source: Survey conducted April 11-17, 2022.
"How Religion Intersects With Americans' Views on the Environment"

PEW RESEARCH CENTER

U.S. Protestants in evangelical and historically Black traditions especially likely to believe humanity is 'living in the end times'

Do you believe we are living in the end times?

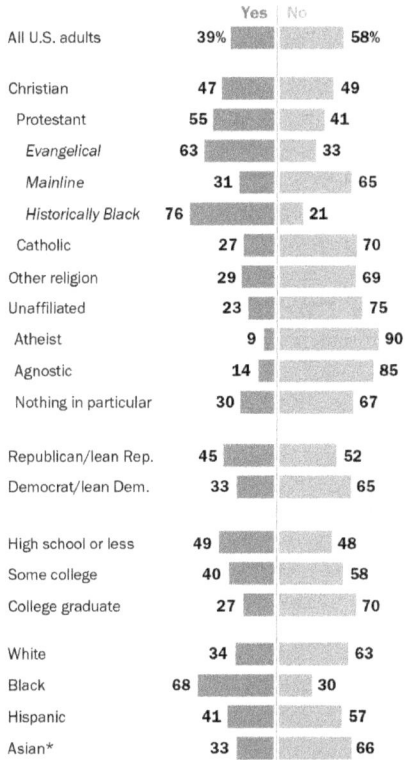

	Yes	No
All U.S. adults	39%	58%
Christian	47	49
Protestant	55	41
Evangelical	63	33
Mainline	31	65
Historically Black	76	21
Catholic	27	70
Other religion	29	69
Unaffiliated	23	75
Atheist	9	90
Agnostic	14	85
Nothing in particular	30	67
Republican/lean Rep.	45	52
Democrat/lean Dem.	33	65
High school or less	49	48
Some college	40	58
College graduate	27	70
White	34	63
Black	68	30
Hispanic	41	57
Asian*	33	66

*Estimates for Asian adults are representative of English speakers only.
Note: Those who did not answer are not shown. White, Black and Asian adults include those who report being only one race and are not Hispanic. Hispanics are of any race. "Other religion" includes those who identify as Jewish, Muslim, Buddhist, Hindu, or with another world religion or other non-Christian faith.
Source: Survey conducted April 11-17, 2022.
"How Religion Intersects with Americans' Views on the Environment"

PEW RESEARCH CENTER

These two *Pew Research Reports* above confirm my suspicions as to the necessity to write this book, *The 70th Week and Rapture Parallels*, because I must warn the Body of Christ by helping them to understand the Biblical End-of-the-Age chronology as God has laid it out for us in Scripture. I want the Body of Christ to be prepared for the future and understand that the anti-Christ has signed the covenant with the Nation of Israel and the many. According to the Scriptures, the 70th Week of Daniel began at the signing of this above-mentioned covenant (Dan 9:27). As you know by now, I believe the signing of that agreement began on September 18-19, 2023 (or effective start date). The anti-Christ can now begin implementing his authority and control through the United Nations SDG7 platform in specific areas that are already in place in our global societies and ready for his authoritative rule. For the majority of this seven-year period, the SDG7 agreement, as I have already pointed out, will eventually include globalization in multiple areas to gain complete control over the entire world. As I have mentioned before, this globalization will include agriculture, which will be necessary in order to control all the food supplies of the world with promises of providing food to all, and the economy — and there will be an era of great economic success. Investors will make huge fortunes all over the financial world, in the beginning. All people who do not have their names written in *The Lamb's Book of Life* will receive the mark of the anti-Christ, which will be required in order to participate in the anti-Christ's global economic financial system. This mandatory participation will be necessary in order to buy or sell anything from anywhere in the world. I have also mentioned earlier that this globalization will also be political. The globalists' Agenda 2030 will give the anti-Christ total rule over the entire world, including the 193 member states of the United Nations and all the BRICS Financial Treaty Members. He will bring together, through the U.N. and Agenda 2030, a political peace that the world has never known, in the beginning. All the nations of the world, through the United Nations SDG7 and the Members of BRICS countries, will be forced to receive the mark of the anti-Christ. This globalization will also be religious. All people will be forced to worship him or be killed. This means that all members of every religion in the world, including Judaism and Christianity, will be forced to worship him or be killed. This is another reason I believe the anti-Christ is a Muslim. The anti-Christ's punishment for disobedience looks identical to the Sharia Law which is derived from the Quran, the Hadith, and the Tawrat (i.e. Torah), and prescribes the death penalty for apostasy and disobedience. Allah's commands must be obeyed. Also, the standard method of execution in Islamic Law is beheading (Surah 2:191; 4:101; 5:17, 51; 47:4). Beheading is the primary way of execution in the Last Days by the anti-Christ (Rev. 20:4). Could it be that the anti-Christ is a Muslim? I think so! Could it be through miraculous signs and wonders that he deceives and convinces many to believe that he is God? Absolutely! There will also be a globalization of social media control. The anti-Christ's globalization of social media may include a consolidated version of Facebook, X (formally Twitter), YouTube, Tik-Tok, WhatsApp, WeChat, Instagram, Snapchat, and Telegram, coupled with a much more advanced surveillance technologically.

The anti-Christ will work in partnership with another demonically-possessed man like himself, who has been identified in Scripture as the false prophet (Rev. 13:11–15). Jesus Christ told us that anti-Christ and the false prophets will rise and show great signs and wonders to deceive, if possible, even the elect (Mt. 24:24). The anti-Christ will blaspheme and boast against the God of Israel. The opinion of this author is that the anti-Christ will be a Muslim because of these six additional reasons, which we find in Scripture and in history:

1. The anti-Christ will hate Jews and Christians. The Quran tells its followers to kill Jews and Christians wherever you find them.[17]
2. The anti-Christ will have no respect for his father's faith. Islam has the same forefather as Judaism — Abraham. Orthodox Judaism is from the bloodline of Isaac, and Islam is from the bloodline of Ishmael.[18]
3. The anti-Christ is a liar and will deny the Jewish God-the-Father and that the Jewish Son of God is the Christ (1 Jn. 2:18-22). In the Quran, Islam denies that God is a Father and has a Son (Surah 4:171; 5:72-75; 116-118).

---

17 The Qur'an -- Surah 2:191; 4:101; 5:17, 51; 9:123.
18 The Qur'an refers to Abraham as the friend of God (4:125). The Qur'an extols Abraham as a model, an exemplar, obedient and not an idolater (16:120). Islam traces their tie to Abraham through his son, Ishmael.

4. The anti-Christ will change the times and laws using Islamic Lunar Calendar and Sharia Law.[19]

5. Islam is the fastest-growing religion in the world and, according to *The Pew Research Report*, could perhaps surpass Christianity by 2060. If this happens, Islam will be the largest and fastest-growing religion in the world by 2060.

6. Islamic eschatology has many similarities with Christian eschatology in that it also has an End-Time era of trials and tribulation. It also has a time of immorality followed by mighty wars. It also has worldwide unnatural phenomena. It also has the Second Coming of Isa (i.e. Jesus), who brings a heavenly victory against the Dajjal (i.e. anti-Christ). Islam also has a resurrection of the dead. I believe that the Islamic Isa is in fact the actual anti-Christ. They reverse Jesus and the anti-Christ in their eschatology.[20] In other words, when the anti-Christ comes, they will think he is Jesus (i.e. Isa), and when Jesus comes, they will think He is the anti-Christ (i.e. Dajjal). Dajjal is an evil figure in Islamic eschatology who they believe will pretend to be the promised Messiah and later claim to be God. To me this completely makes sense and is consistent with Biblical eschatology.[21]

Also, we must understand that Jesus (Mt. 24:21-22), Daniel (Da. 12:1), Jeremiah (Jer. 30:6-7), Luke (chapter 21), Mark (chapter 13), John (Rev. 7:14), and others all prophesied about the Great Tribulation, Jacob's Trouble, and a Time of Trouble. They are using different names in describing the same event. Although we do not know the day or the hour of Christ's Return, we do know the season. The reason we know the season is that Jesus told us certain signs would occur prior to His Second Coming. Jesus also said that when we see these signs appear, His Second Coming is near — right at the door (Mt.24:33). Here I want to mention once again the signs that Christ discussed with His disciples: there will be false Christ's and false prophets,

19 Daniel 7:25.
20 The Qur'an; Sunnah literature.
21 Dr. Shazia Siddiqi (17 January 2020). *"The Antichrist of Islamic Tradition"*. *Olean Times Herald*; Farhang, Mehrvash (2017). "Dajjal". In Madelung, Wilferd; Daftary, Farhad (eds.) *Encyclopedia Islamica*. Translated by Negahban, Farzin. Leiden and Boston; Brill Publishers.

wars and rumors of wars, pestilence, famine, earthquakes, and death, all occurring slowly and gradually like birth pains prior to His return. The birth pains are events and trends that are occurring now and will continue to occur on the earth prior to Jesus' Return. Birth pains have been occurring on earth for a very long time, but they are increasing gradually and will continue to increase until Christ's Second Coming. During this final generation prior to the Lord's return, these birth pains will have greater intensity than ever before as time progresses forward. In this final generation before the Lord's return, the birth pains aligned with the opening of the first seven Seals of Revelation 6:1-8:5 (Mt. 24:4-8; Mk. 13:5-8; Lk. 21:8-11). The seven-year covenant that was signed between the anti-Christ (i.e. the United Nations), Israel, and the many on September 18-19 (or effective date) shows us the current generation is the last generation — which means all the signs that Christ mentioned to His disciples began prior to the actual signing of the covenant. You see, the signs did not begin at the moment of the signing of this covenant, but rather they already gradually began prior to the signing of the covenant, but at a lesser intensity, and have continued to increase in their intensity gradually since the signing of the covenant and will increase until Christ's Return. It is easy to see we are currently experiencing the birth pains in our daily lives. All we have to do is turn on the television or go on the internet or listen to the radio, and we can see and hear about false Christs, false prophets, famines, pestilence, plagues, and earthquakes. Not only do we see all these signs mentioned by Christ in our everyday reality, but we can clearly see they are increasing and intensifying as well.[22] There is no doubt in my mind we are in the beginning of The 70th Week of Daniel today.

---

22   https://www.reliefweb.int/disasters; https://www.reliefweb.int/earthquakes; https://www.disasterphilanthropy.org/disasters.

The 70th-Week of Daniel's Chronological Order

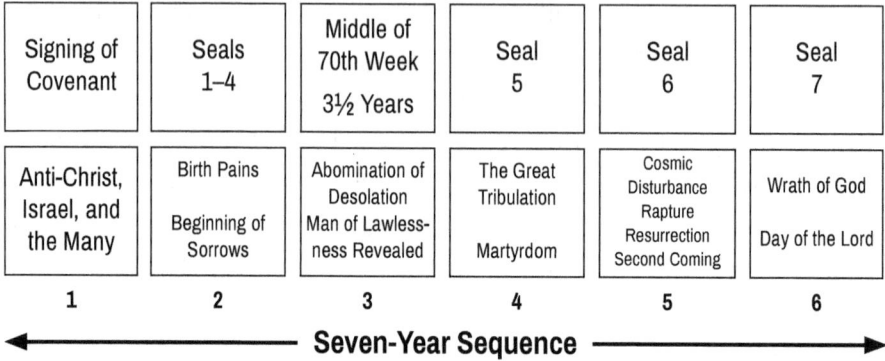

Signing of Covenant	Seals 1–4	Middle of 70th Week 3½ Years	Seal 5	Seal 6	Seal 7
Anti-Christ, Israel, and the Many	Birth Pains Beginning of Sorrows	Abomination of Desolation Man of Lawlessness Revealed	The Great Tribulation Martyrdom	Cosmic Disturbance Rapture Resurrection Second Coming	Wrath of God Day of the Lord
1	2	3	4	5	6

◄─────────── **Seven-Year Sequence** ───────────►

I know there will be those who will read *The 70th-Week & Rapture Parallels* and not accept the 70th-Week-Hypothesis chapter as being valid. I understand there will be people who will disregard the signing of the U.N. SDG7 seven-year aggressive agreement by itself as evidence for the beginning of The 70th-Week-of-Daniel Prophecies' fulfillment, relative to the covenant between the anti-Christ, the Nation of Israel, and the many, even though the SDG7 agreement is a seven-year agreement between the United Nation, Israel and the 193 member states. I understand this evidence, for some, is not sufficient as proof, but if my 70th-Week Hypothesis is correct, we can expect to see the constructing of the New Temple in Jerusalem sometime between the first and fourth Seals, but probably closer to the second Seal of the Book of Revelation. The building of the Temple could begin at any time now since September 18-19, 2023 (or effective date), but has to be built well before the fifth Seal occurs. When you see and/or hear on the news — and you will — the announcement that the New Temple is being built in Jerusalem, then the evidence the 70th-Week of Daniel has begun will have been verified; but if the New Temple does not get built well before the fifth Seal, or the 3-½-year midpoint, then my 70th-Week Hypothesis is false and should be immediately discarded. But again if my hypothesis is correct, then you will absolutely witness these three events listed below simultaneously occurring within a 3-½-year time period as confirmation of the validity of this hypothesis (Daniel 9:25-27). And I want to add that, of course, I would hope you would have validated this hypothesis at the building of the Third Temple in Jerusalem, in order to allow you more time for preparation:

1. The signing of the seven-year SDG7 aggressive agreement[23] between the anti-Christ (i.e. United Nations), The Nation of Israel, and the many (i.e. 193 U.N. member states) indeed initiated Daniel's 70th Week.
2. The building of the New Jewish Temple in Jerusalem some time at the beginning of Daniel's 70th Week, probably closer to the second Seal.
3. The revealing of the anti-Christ's identity at the 3-½-year midpoint of Daniel's 70th Week.

The fulfillment of the three prophetic events mentioned above occurring simultaneously clearly would confirm this hypothesis as valid, but I do believe that we can achieve a reasonable and positive validation at the building of the Third Temple in Jerusalem solely based on the evidence of its mathematical probability!

IT IS MY EDUCATED AND WELL-RESEARCHED OPINION that, through the United Nation Agenda 2030 (SDG7) platform, the 70th Week of Daniel indeed began on September 18-19, 2023 (or effective start date).[24] The United Nation Agenda 30 (SDG7) platform for sustainable development is clearly being marketed as a rescue operation for people and the planet. It contains 17 goals that 193 member states (including Israel and the U.S.) have pledged to aggressively secure. The SDG7 agreement is an extremely complex and difficult-to-follow, wordy document that focuses on the idea of a global partnership to eradicate problems related to global human rights, poverty, and the environment. Here are the five critical dimensions, or the five "P's" of Agenda 30: 1.) people, 2.) prosperity, 3.) planet, 4.) partnership, and 5.) peace. *The Global Goals and the Agenda 30 Sustainable Development seek to end poverty and hunger, realize the human rights*

---

23   Hebrew *"gabar,"* word in English: and he shall "confirm" — in Strong's Concordance #1396, meaning: to be strong and mighty. It is Interesting that the Agenda 30 SDG7 language uses the word *aggressive* in their description of the SDG7 agreement on their website.

24   https://www.populationmatters.org; https://www.thegiin.org; https://www.undp.org; https://www.unfpa.org/resources/tramsforming-our-world-2030-agenda-sustainable-development; https://www.pif.gov.sa; https://www.sdgs.un.org/2030 agenda; https:www.vision2030.gov.sa; https://www.cccco.edu/About-Us/Vision-2030; https://www.vision2030.org; https://www.unsdg.un.org; https://www.globalgoals.org; https://www.ymca-int/what-we-do/vision-2030; https://www.sdg.iisd.org/news/un-secretary-generals-report-outlines-rescue-plan-for-people-and-planet/; https://www.rumble.com/vpgahd-some-people-are-completely-unaware-of-this-action-plan.html; https://www.sustainabledevelopment.un.org/content/documents/Agenda21.pdf; https://www.rforresistance.wordpress.com/2021/05/01/depopulation-by-injection-the-return-of-fascism-in-europe-and- agenda-2030/.

of all, achieve gender equality and the empowerment of all women and girls, and ensure the lasting protection of the planet and its natural resources." What does this all mean really? Let's take a closer look at the 17 Goals of Agenda 30. Let's decode or compare the 17 Goals of Sustainable Development to see what they actually mean in practice. **Goal 1:** End poverty in all its forms everywhere. **Translation:** Redistribute wealth and resources to make the super-rich wealthier and the middle class poorer; have centralized banks, International Monetary Fund (IMF), world banks, and Federal Reserve to control all finances, and digital one-world currency in a cashless society. **Goal 2:** End hunger, achieve food security, improve nutrition, and promote sustainable agriculture. **Translation:** Use GMOs fortified with synthetic vitamins and minerals, creating disease and causing depopulation. **Goal 3:** Ensure healthy lives and promote wellbeing for all at all ages. **Translation:** Mandate mass vaccination for all children and adults, medicate children, and remove parental freedom, privacy, and responsibility. **Goal 4:** Ensure inclusive and equitable quality education and promote lifelong learning opportunities for all. **Translation:** Socially engineer children to conform to politically correct agendas, standardize and dumb down the curriculum to produce adults incapable of independent thought, distribute U.N. propaganda, and brainwash through compulsory education from cradle to grave. **Goal 5:** Achieve gender equality and empower all women and girls. **Translation:** Promote LGBTQ and feminist agendas; marginalize families, heterosexuality, men, and boys; obtain population control through forced "family planning." **Goal 6:** Ensure available and sustainable management of water and sanitation for all. **Translation:** Privatize all water sources and have all water, including rivers and wells on private land, be controlled by corporations, local government, or states. Of course, they will most likely add fluoride. **Goal 7:** Ensure access to affordable, reliable, sustainable, and modern energy for all. **Translation:** Increase taxes on traditional fuels and institute usage caps for every household, utilize monitoring by health-destroying smart grid with smart meters on everything, and charge peak pricing. **Goal 8:** Promote sustainable, inclusive, and economic growth with full and productive employment and decent work for all. **Translation:** Mandate minimum wages, compliance, and certification; introduce employment quotas that discriminate against the best qualified person for the job; and have Trans-Pacific Partnership (TPP) and a free-trade zone that favor mega corporate interests. **Goal 9:** Build resilient infrastructure and sustainable industrialization and foster innovation. **Translation:** Have toll roads, push public transit, remove free travel, and enforce environmental restrictions. **Goal 10:** Reduce inequality within and among countries. **Translation:** Push international trade agreements on all countries to benefit mega corporations and have even more regional government bureaucracy. **Goal 11:** Make cities and human settlements inclusive, safe, resilient, and sustainable. **Translation**: Create protected rural spaces, forcing people into cities or mega cities with 24/7 surveillance in all public places; ban single-family homes with gardens; and have a "Big Brother," big data surveillance state. **Goal 12:** Ensure sustainable consumption and production patterns. **Translation:** Introduce utility quotas and penalize waste disposal. **Goal 13:** Take urgent action to combat climate change and its impact. **Translation:** Implement carbon footprint taxes/credits. **Goal 14:** Conserve and sustainably use the oceans, seas, and marine resources for sustainable development. **Translation:** Mandate licenses and quotas for all fishing, including individuals who fish for their own consumption; and enforce environmental restrictions to control all oceans, including mineral rights from ocean floors. **Goal 15:** Protect, restore, and promote sustainable use of terrestrial ecosystems; sustainably manage forests; combat desertification; halt and reverse land degradation; and stop biodiversity loss. **Translation:** Ensure that every possible seed is preserved in the global seed vault so that the powers that be can regenerate the earth for themselves, enforce more environmental restrictions, and have more control of resources and mineral rights. **Goal 16:** Promote peaceful and inclusive societies for sustainable development; provide access to justice for all; and build effective, accountable, and inclusive institutions at all levels. **Translation:** Strengthen police state everywhere, gain more control over a region, and remove the Second Amendment of the United States Constitution. **Goal 17:** Strengthen the means of implementation and revitalize the global partnership for sustainable development. **Translation:** Remove national sovereignty worldwide and place every country under a social communist rule of a totalitarian one-world government; promote globalism under the anti-Christ's authority and the bureaucracy of the U.N. Of course these goals are unattainable, but that is beside the point since the anti-Christ's real agenda is not to improve the world, but to control it.

The Logical Conclusion of the 70th-Week Hypothesis

If indeed my 70th-Week Hypothesis is correct, then what would the logical outworking of such a conclusion mean? The correct, final conclusion would mean the premise and all the Scripture references in this book would be rendered correct and true, and the 17 Sustainable Development Goals began to be implemented (according to the U.N. SDG7 Summit) on September 18-19, 2023 (or effective date), and will continue for the next seven years, and will conclude either by physical death caused by war, pestilence, plague, famine, or martyrdom or by the Second Coming of Jesus Christ and the Rapture at the sixth Seal (Rev. 6:12-13). I believe that Agenda 30 (SDG7) is a platform of diplomacy for the anti-Christ's covert operation, in the beginning, by which he can achieve his one-world-government and authoritative rule. Remember, he has a crown and a bow with no arrows (Rev. 6:1-2). This is why the Bible tells us that his identity will remain a mystery until he is revealed through the Abomination of Desolation (Mt. 24:15; 2 Th. 2:3-4), which means that the anti-Christ's identity will not be specifically known by the world in general until the middle of Daniel's 70-th Week — 3-½ years after its commencement.

Terrible Times Are Coming!

The Apostle Paul, in 2 Timothy, provides us a detailed description of the terrible End-Times' condition of society that has already gradually arrived, like Birth Pains, to planet Earth. We read the following passage:

2 Timothy 3:1-5

> *"¹But understand this: In the last days terrible times will come. ²For men will be lovers of themselves, lovers of money, boastful, arrogant, abusive, disobedient to their parents, ungrateful, unholy, ³unloving, unforgiving, slanderous, without self-control, brutal, without love of good, ⁴traitorous, reckless, conceited, lovers of pleasure rather than lovers of God, ⁵having a form of godliness but denying its power. Turn away from such as these!"*

Does the above description of Paul's End-Time society sound at all familiar to you? It does to me! I think the question we should be asking ourselves is, "How can we turn away from a society such as this and live faithfully to God during these Last Days? Living faithfully in the Last Days will require at least these six responses that are keys to enduring the tests and trials that we will experience in the 70th Week of Daniel through God's grace:

1. Rejoicing and giving thanks!
2. Reading, believing, and acting on the Word of God!
3. Crying out to God in prayer!
4. Overcoming evil with good!
5. Fasting!
6. Sharing the Gospel with a lost and dying world!

In Christ,

David Wayne Meeker

The views and opinions expressed in this book, *The 70th-Week & Rapture Parallels*, are those of the author, although they are based on and substantiated by Scripture; they do not reflect the views of the majority of the Christian Church — yet!

Scriptures About Jesus and His Second Coming

Matthew 16:27; 25:1-13, 31-46; 26:64.

Mark 8:38; 14:62.

Luke 9:26; 12:40; 18:8; 21:25-28.

John 3:16-18; 5:22, 28-29; 6:39-40; 14:1-3; 16:33.

Acts 1:9-11; 3:19-21; 17:31.

1 Corinthians 4:5; 11:26.

Philippians 1:6, 10; 3:20-21; 4:5.

Colossians 3:4.

1 Thessalonians 1:10; 2:19-20; 3:13; 4:13-18; 5:1-3, 23.

2 Thessalonians 2:1-2, 8.

1 Timothy 6:13-16.

2 Timothy 4:8.

Titus 2:11-14.

Hebrews 9:28; 10:24-25, 37.

James 5:7-9.

1 Peter 1:3-5, 13; 2:24; 4:7, 13.

1 John 2:28; 3:2-3.

Jude 1:14-15.

Revelation 3:11; 16:15, 17-21; 20:11-15; 22:12, 20.

How to Become a Christian

1. Admit

Admit to God that you are a sinner. Repent, and turn away from your sin.

- Romans 3:23 – *"for all have sinned and fall short of the glory of God,"*
- Romans 3:24 – *"and are justified by his grace as a gift, through the redemption that is in Christ Jesus."*
- Romans 6:23 – *"For the wages of sin is death, but the free gift of God is eternal life in Christ Jesus our Lord."*
- Acts 3:19 – *"Repent therefore, and turn again, that your sins may be blotted out."*
- 1 John 1:9 – *"If we confess our sins, he is faithful and just to forgive us our sins and to cleanse us from all unrighteousness."*

2. Believe

Believe that Jesus Christ is God's Son, and accept God's gift of forgiveness from sin.

- John 3:16 – *"For God so loved the world, that he gave his only Son, that whoever believes in him should not perish but have eternal life."*
- John 3:17 – *"For God did not send his Son into the world to condemn the world, but in order that the world might be saved through him."*
- John 3:18 – *"Whoever believes in him is not condemned, but whoever does not believe is condemned already, because he has not believed in the name of the only Son of God."*
- John 14:6 – *"Jesus said to him, 'I am the way, and the truth, and the life. No one comes to the Father except through me.'"*
- Acts 4:12 – *"And there is salvation in no one else, for there is no other name under heaven given among men by which we must be saved."*
- Romans 5:8 – *"but God shows his love for us in that while we were still sinners, Christ died for us."*
- Ephesians 2:8 – *"For by grace you have been saved through faith. And this is not your own doing; it is the gift of God,"*
- Ephesians 2:9 – *"not a result of works, so that no one may boast."*
- John 1:11 – *"He came to his own, and his own people did not receive him."*
- John 1:12 – *"But to all who did receive him, who believed in his name, he gave the right to become children of God,"*
- John 1:13 – *"who were born, not of blood nor of the will of the flesh nor of the will of man, but of God."*

3. Confess

Confess your faith in Jesus Christ as Savior and Lord.

- Romans 10:9 – *"because, if you confess with your mouth that Jesus is Lord and believe in your heart that God raised him from the dead, you will be saved."*
- Romans 10:10 – *"For with the heart one believes and is justified, and with the mouth one confesses and is saved."*
- Romans 10:13 – *"For 'everyone who calls on the name of the Lord will be saved.'"*

Notes

_____

_____

_____

_____

_____

_____

_____

_____

_____

_____

_____

_____

_____

_____

_____

_____

Notes

Notes

_____

_____

_____

_____

_____

_____

_____

_____

_____

_____

_____

_____

_____

_____

_____

_____

Notes

Notes

Please contact us at lastchancemusic1@aol.com if you need a Bible and we will send you one at no cost. The price has been paid in full.

Do you want to help support Last Chance Music Ministry in reaching a lost and dying world? Buy our products so we can continue reaching the lost for Christ — before this seven-year opportunity passes!

Deepen your relationship with God through a better understanding of His Word using these LCMM materials (through our books and music) that glorify God, edify the Body of Christ, and reach a lost and dying world. Purchase these LCMM products below — available now!

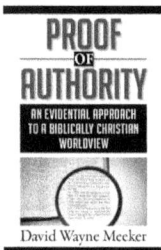

Proof of Authority: An Evidential Approach to a Biblically Christian Worldview The premise of this book is that Biblical Christianity is the only religion in the world that provides with its message *Proof of Authority*. God gives us overwhelming internal and external evidence in the coherency, accuracy, and unity of His Word as it relates to our reality in validating His message. God does not expect His creation to follow Him blindly, but rather He gives us overwhelming proof of His authority.

Proof of Authority — available in hardcover, softcover, and eBook. Category: Worldviews (334 pages). Available at Amazon.com.

In Christ's Service: A Concise Biblical Approach. Here is a book that gives answers to questions such as these: What does it mean to be a disciple? How can I please God with my Life? How can I get closer to God? Is obedience important to God? Should I share my faith with others? This book can help you better understand what it means to be a follower of Christ! *In Christ's Service* is available only in an eBook format from digital book download sites, including Amazon.com, Kobo.com, Barnes and Noble, BookBaby.com, Scribd. com, Booktopia.com, and many more! Category: Discipleship (142 pages).

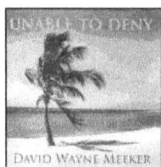

Unable to Deny CD; music available for digital downloads only. Category: Christian Music. 10 songs total — all originals. Available at digital music download sites, including Apple Music, Amazon.com, Pandora, Shazam, Spotify, Youtube, Boomplay Music, Google Play, and many more!

Laura Landers CD; music available at Amazon.com and Apple Music. Category: Christian Music. 12 songs total — all originals. Laura had this album recorded before we got married and is one of my favorites!